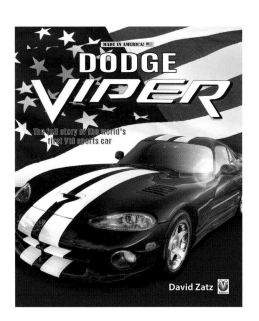

Also from Veloce Publishing

Find many more titles at: www.veloce.co.uk

First published in October 2020 by Veloce Publishing Limited, Veloce House, Parkway Farm Business Park, Middle Farm Way, Poundbury, Dorchester DT1 3AR, England. Tel +44 (0)1305 260068 / Fax 01305 250479 / e-mail info@veloce.co.uk / web www.velocebooks.com.
ISBN: 978-1-787115-29-3; UPC: 6-36847-01529-9.

MADE IN AMERICA!

DODGE
VIPER

The full story of the world's
first V10 sports car

David Zatz

VELOCE

Contents

Acknowledgements

First, I must thank my wife, Katherine, and my kids, Zoe and Ben, for their encouragement and support.

Team Viper brought us a stunning car, while helping Chrysler to change the look and feel of America's large cars, minivans, pickups, and sport-utilities. François Castaing, Bob Lutz, Roy Sjoberg, and Team Viper not only created the Viper, but helped to turn around Chrysler itself, then told people how they did it.

Roy Sjoberg answered my left-field questions quickly and honestly, as he has for Viper fans for years. Other members of Team Viper have told their stories to the public over and over, helping to illuminate the early days.

Jon Brobst of ViperPartsRack.com provided information, insight, and photos, and caught errors in the draft. Maurice Liang, a founding member and current writer/photographer for the Viper Owners Association, provided photos and a good deal of help, even though his third Viper book debuted as I was writing this one. Marc Rozman, respected and retired Chrysler dyno technician, provided many, many photos without question or hesitation.

Speaking of photos, I have to thank Angela Puckett (Treasurer of the Viper Club of America), Allpar's Patrick Rall and Jeremy White, and full-time professional photographer Jerry Mendoza for sharing their photography. The photos in this book are copyrighted by the photographers; please contact them directly with any reproduction requests.

FCA US LLC's legal team worked quickly to clear the use of photos, information, and the Dodge and Viper names in this book (Viper, Dodge, and SRT are registered trademarks of FCA US, which is part of Fiat Chrysler Automobiles). People from both the Viper Owners Association and Viper Club of America helped with this book and are helping to keep the cars on the track.

Warren 'Bob' Steele, Roy's stepbrother, helped me with Chrysler material long before this book, and provided amusing stories which Roy later confirmed. Finally, retired engineer Robert W Sheaves grounded me in automotive engineering; J P Joans hooked me up with information; and Tim Nevinson at Veloce was helpful and understanding.

Only one name is on the cover, but this book is the product of a wide-ranging, helpful group of people, and I thank all of them.

David Zatz

1

Dodge becomes a performance brand

Inseparable brothers John and Horace Dodge started with a machinist shop, made a fortune making bicycles, built engines for Ransom Olds, and, finally, lent Henry Ford enough money, skill, material, and labor to get Ford's third car (his first successful one) into production. In 1914, they started building their own cars under the Dodge Brothers name.

The brothers worked hard and partied hard; their cars reflected the 'work hard' side. Durable and well-engineered, Dodge Brothers cars quickly garnered a good reputation and high sales (the word 'dependability' came from their ad campaign). The brothers did not make performance cars or, for the most part, trucks; ironically, their name would end up being associated mainly with performance cars and trucks.

Both Dodge brothers died in 1920. Eight years later, Chrysler bought the Dodge Brothers company, phasing out the existing designs and the word 'Brothers' in the name. For years, Dodge was a midline car that shared heavily with Plymouth, DeSoto, and Chrysler.

The brand's first high-performance car was, arguably, the 1956 D-500, backed by high-performance V8 engines. The D-500 broke numerous speed records and, with its upgraded suspension, could run at either the drag strip or a road race; but Plymouth had a similar car, the Fury, debut in the same year. Plymouth was still the go-to brand of NASCAR legends Lee and Richard Petty, and the creator of the Barracuda, Road Runner, and Duster low-budget/high-performance cars. Dodge, at least, was first with aero-cars for NASCAR speedways: the Charger 500 and Charger Daytona.

When he took over Chrysler, Lee Iacocca limited Plymouth to value vehicles, while Dodge had the Shelby-modified cars – and the Turbo III engine which made the Dodge Spirit R/T the fastest sedan in America. Ultimately, though, Dodge's image as a muscle brand was cemented by the ultimate American performance car: the Viper.

Every Viper, no matter how much well-crafted Alcantara leather or cost-conscious fabric was wrapped around the seats, had a few key qualities. It was raw and brutal, pure in performance. People who may not have cared that much about cars took a Viper for a spin and fell in love, and people who already loved sports cars fell deeper in love. The force of the Viper was something to be reckoned with, and it was rare in any car near its price; but it was coupled with European-style cornering strength. It was a uniquely American interpretation of performance, dominated by torque, backed by superb cornering.

The Viper show car appeared in 1989, when the Plymouth Reliant K-car and Dodge Omni compacts were still huge sellers, and the last traditional Chrysler Corporation rear-wheel drive car was in its final year. It turned around Dodge's and Chrysler's image; without the Viper, there would be no Dodge Challenger Hellcat, no Demon, no Redeye. Once that big V10 pushed its way into Dodge's catalog, no number of minivans would take away its stamp.

This 1922 Dodge Brothers car belongs to Tom Buss. It's sturdy, reliable, and not especially sporty. (Author)

2

Creating the concept car

There are a few Dodge Viper creation stories, as befits a car everyone would want to be associated with, but every version has the same players.

We can start with former Marine Bob Lutz, 'Maximum Bob.' Lutz was known for his strong opinions, strongly expressed, but some claimed that anyone who made a strong argument could change his mind – not necessarily a common trait among executives.

François Castaing had run Renault's racing program before becoming the head of engineering at Renault's American Motors (AMC). After Chrysler bought AMC from Renault in 1987, Castaing was pivotal in getting Chrysler to adopt AMC's methods for car development. That brought dramatic changes in the company's product line, and a reversal from 'risking bankruptcy' to 'most profitable automaker.' Castaing was unsatisfied with 'good enough' solutions and wanted to permanently end any image of Chrysler as being behind the times.

Tom Gale was Chrysler's head of design, the owner of a rare AAR 'Cuda, and a well-liked manager known for bringing out the best in designers; he fought a losing battle to rebuild Plymouth, while helping Chrysler to gain a reputation for good styling and design. He believed that each brand needed a focal car to define its essence; Jeep had the Wrangler, Dodge would get the Viper, and Plymouth eventually had the Prowler (they never did get one for Chrysler).

Finally, the chief executive, Lee Iacocca, had famously saved Chrysler, cutting through red tape and paralyzing bureaucracy with instant decisions and firm edicts. During his first years at Chrysler, he pushed through the highly profitable minivans and convertibles, along with some other cars best forgotten. Lee had a dramatic impact on quality, though he pushed for cars to be delivered early and cheaply as well – contradictory demands that some managers handled better than others.

In the early 1980s, following fuel shortages, price hikes, and government fuel-efficiency rules, Lee Iacocca focused on four-cylinder, front-wheel-drive cars, and was slowly phasing out the truck business. The strategy was right at the time, but then gas prices stayed low, and government

Bob Lutz with the media, in 2012. (Author)

Tom Gale in 2004. (Courtesy Marc Rozman)

restrictions were lifted. His insistence on saving pennies and diverting resources to buy other companies led to recycling the same architectures and parts over and over, hurting Chrysler's reputation.

There are a few versions of what followed, but they are essentially minor variations of the same story.

According to one executive, Bob Lutz convinced Iacocca to develop a new, class-leading pickup truck, which would become the 1994 Dodge Ram 1500. The main attraction of the 1980s Dodge pickups was their diesel engine; buyers said they had "a Cummins diesel with a Dodge wrapped around it." Neither GM nor Ford had matched the Cummins diesel, and they might not try to match a gasoline V10, either. It would be another engine to wrap Dodges around, if nothing else.

To save time and money, the ten-cylinder would be based on the company's 360ci (5.9L) V8, whose family dated back around three decades; one could even argue that it was based on Chrysler's very first V8s. Lutz was reportedly told that the engine would be too rough, and asked Jeep/Truck Engineering's François Castaing to look into it. Castaing checked it out, and told Lutz that the V10 would work well; despite its odd timing and V8-based architecture, it was indeed smooth at idle. During that brief meeting, the executives ruminated on the possibility that the V10 would power a low-volume European sports car, like the Facel Vega, Jensen, or Bristol; the Bristol Beaufighter, Beaufort, Britannia, Brigand, and Blenheim all used Chrysler's 360 V8.

Castaing and Lutz talked about European sports cars with American V8s on a Friday. The following Monday, Lutz called in Tom Gale, the head of design, to move things forward. Gale and his team had already done a sports car concept, the Izod, which was more of an influence on the company's version of the Mitsubishi Eclipse, but also sent some of its form to the Viper.

Bob Lutz told a different version to Daniel F Carney (in his 2001 book *Dodge Viper*), saying he felt uncomfortable taking his Shelby Cobra to work at Chrysler because it used a Ford V8. He rejected the idea of swapping in a Chrysler V8, because the most powerful V8 Chrysler of the time was a truck motor. The story is a little ingenuous; Lutz could have gone to any one of Chrysler's high-performance small engines, or followed Bristol's example by retuning the truck motor. In any case, Lutz claimed that's when he thought of creating a brand new concept car, using the V10 and New Venture manual transmission being developed for the Ram pickup.

Lutz turned to Jeep/Truck Engineering leader François Castaing for the next step, because, he said, the car guys were too busy; but he might have been thinking about how the truck guys, infused with Jeep people from the 1987 acquisition, were more open to new ideas. AMC's Cherokee and Comanche had been almost revolutionary in the SUV and pickup world, yet they were built with few resources. François Castaing had racing experience and knew how to perform miracles with limited funds.

Tom Gale's story was that the three of them had been talking about doing a sports car for a while, and one day Lutz asked why they didn't just do it. Perhaps that was why Tom Gale already had several designs in the studio; the go-ahead from Lutz and Castaing meant that he and his people could explore those designs further, and, after the group chose one drawing in particular, Gale put his staff to work on half-scale packages. The speed with which Gale provided renderings probably surprised the others.

All these stories follow a similar path, with relatively minor differences. Chrysler was working on a V10, and Lutz, Castaing, and Gale all knew about world-class sports cars from smaller automakers that used American engines, and they took the concept to its natural conclusion.

Tom Gale with the Chrysler-developed 1987 Lamborghini Portofino concept, which influenced the entire Dodge lineup for years. This 2014 photo, taken at the Chrysler Museum, includes the Viper concept in the background. (Courtesy Marc Rozman)

Lee Iacocca after receiving the American Patriot Award in 2010. (Courtesy Hemi Andersen)

*Carroll Shelby with Viper enthusiast Jon Brobst at the 2003 'Viper vs Viper' airshow race.
(Courtesy Jon Brobst)*

British automaker Jensen had taken a high-tech route to Chrysler-V8-plus-European-body, especially with the four-wheel-drive FF; but Castaing, Lutz, and Gale felt they should have a simpler car, something along the lines of the Shelby Cobra, which was an English AC Cobra adapted to an American V8.

The car would be technologically sophisticated, not in terms of feature lists (turbochargers, antilock brakes, etc), but in its lightweight materials, advanced construction techniques, and computer-aided design. The car would have just enough space for a driver and passenger, and the engine would be as far back as possible, pushing into the cabin – creating "truly heroic proportions," in Gale's words.

The sports car would still be built around the upcoming V10 engine and five-speed transmission, using some Dodge Dakota parts for the suspension and rear axle, to cut costs. No matter how well Chrysler might be doing at the moment, it had limited resources that Iacocca had, through unwise acquisitions, spread rather thinly. If they could use off-the-shelf parts, they could sell at a reasonable price, and within a reasonable time. Indeed, the $70 million budget Castaing had in mind was not

much more than the budget for converting the Plymouth Voyager into the Chrysler Town & Country by making some appearance changes and adding nicer trim.

Why not just have Iacocca's friends Shelby or DeTomaso design and build the car? Castaing pointed out that they would not learn anything from that; part of the project's rationale was to shake up the engineering groups and learn more about advanced materials. What's more, a sports car built by someone else would not change Chrysler's image any more than the Bristol Beaufighter had.

Before the three could go to production, they needed a concept car to help convince Lee Iacocca to lay out the money. Then they could round up around 70 people to develop the car, within three years (in a company whose normal cycle time was closer to five), for around $70 million – a small budget for revising an existing car, much less creating an entirely new one.

Lutz allegedly wanted to use the Cobra name, but was blocked by Ford's lawyers – not that Castaing, Gale, or Iacocca would likely have thought that name to be a good idea. 'Challenger' was reportedly floated. The name 'Viper' was, though, universally accepted; likewise, when

The first Viper logo, to be dubbed 'Sneaky Pete.'
(Courtesy Marc Rozman)

one designer sketched an emblem, the team instantly agreed on it.

The goal was to unveil the concept at the January 1989 North American International Auto Show in Detroit; and it was already mid-1988. Tom Gale pushed and got a full-size clay in just six weeks, a fast turnaround. For speed and secrecy, Gale had the chassis and suspension built by Boyd Coddington's shop, while the body was put together by Metalcrafters; normally they would use the company's facilities in Highland Park, Michigan.

Bob Lutz was surprised when he saw the model, because of the speed and the level of development; he had envisioned a more direct copy of the Cobra, and this was, in his words, "a totally unique car … as opposed to being 'son of Cobra.'"

The show car wouldn't need to be functional, but Chrysler, at the time, favored working concepts. Former engine chief Willem Weertman, in his book *Chrysler Engines*, stated that a V10 was taken from the truck program; it was an experiment, built out of two 360ci V8s with a fabricated crank. Gale also had a %-scale Viper built with a V8; it can be spotted by the lack of a 'sport bar' behind the seats. The V10 show car could be driven, but it could only turn the front wheels by a few degrees, and

Concept car at the Walter P Chrysler museum. (Author)

there was no wheelhouse protection from rain or road water – everything was open, according to Warren Steele.

Dodge had the fastest four-door sedan in America in the Spirit R/T, but the boxy five-passenger sedan failed to win much love or attention. Magazine writers had decided Chrysler was no longer capable of advanced engineering, crediting any innovations to outside suppliers, largely because of all the K-car reworkings. It was all the more shocking, then, when Chrysler put the Viper onto a rotating display at the show. It was incredibly popular, even though it was only a concept with no promise of production; one Team Viper engineer claimed people were stacked 12 deep, trying to get a look at it.

Popular Mechanic's Jim Dunne wrote that it was "classic simplicity personified," with a "[Jaguar] XKE-like front end, Cobra rear … and five exhaust headers snaking through a break in the front fender." He added that it "can't help but stir the blood of any sports car aficionado," and wrote that the powertrain, at least, would be in production soon. Dunne also predicted, or learned, that if it was greenlighted for production, it could be available as early as 1992.

The Viper concept used a new variation of a venerable engine with a tried-and-true architecture, but it clearly announced that some people in the company were ready to go beyond K-cars. Putting it into production would be a much more powerful statement.

The production car had another center gauge. (Courtesy Marc Rozman, from Eyes on Design 2018)

A closer look at the dashboard. (Author)

Functional side pipes on the 1989 concept car. (Marc Rozman)

The 1989 concept, in motion. (Courtesy Marc Rozman)

3

Putting the Viper into production

François Castaing recalled that he convinced Lee Iacocca and Bob Lutz to put the Viper into production by casting it as a technical and training exercise, rather than a simple car project. This way, they could build skills within the company – skills that had been blunted by too many years of recycled architectures – and indoctrinate engineers in different ways of working. (The main change would be shifting to a platform team; more on that later.) Indeed, the company had contracted out its convertibles to ASC, and some of its sportier cars to Shelby Enterprises, rather than doing them in-house. It was time to rebuild.

GETTING THE GREEN LIGHT

To simplify the full process, the Viper needed two approvals, one for a production prototype and one for actual production cars. The latter would arrive about halfway through the program.

To get approval for the prototype, François Castaing, Tom Gale, and Bob Lutz started bringing people together to convince Lee Iacocca to move forward. They brought Iacocca's friend, Carroll Shelby, onboard; Shelby didn't think much of the V10 idea, thinking the car would be far too heavy to corner well. Lutz, though, insisted that engine was needed to set the car apart.

Carroll Shelby may have been key to the process; he and Iacocca had been friends for many years, and Iacocca tended to be loyal to his friends. Lutz hired Shelby on as an advisor to the project; Shelby remembered Lutz calling it "something like the old 427 Cobra, only a 1990s version."

One interesting outcome was described by Joel W Jackson, in his book *Fast Days* (about working at Shelby Enterprises). He wrote that Carroll Shelby ordered him to make a "Cobra of the nineties" with a round tube chassis, the 'stump puller' (V10 truck engine) in front, a ZF transmission from a De Tomaso Pantera, and Corvette front spindles. The body was styled by a local artist; the chassis and suspension were made by Frank 'Monty' Montgomery, Bob Brizinski, and Joel Jackson. (The Pantera eventually sold with a Dodge V8 engine, modified and endowed with twin turbochargers, and without a transmission.)

If Joel Jackson's story is true, and there's no reason to believe it isn't, Shelby assumed that Chrysler would eventually delegate the car to him. However, Castaing, Lutz, and Gale knew that a Shelby car using a Chrysler engine would not help them much in terms of publicity, morale, or skill-building; they also probably wanted to build in larger numbers than Shelby could. Regardless of the timing, Carroll Shelby helped the Viper project leader with informal advice and support, and continued to support it with Lee Iacocca.

The Viper was not all that much of a risk, even to the cash-poor Chrysler Corporation. For around $70 million, it would guarantee magazine covers and press attention as the most expensive (and fastest) American car, with the biggest American engine, either by cubic inches or by cylinder count. It would challenge cars that cost twice as much from world-renowned automakers, and conquer the Corvette on the track. That would garner showroom traffic no number of television commercials could provide, save Chrysler from slapping a lot of money onto a lot of hoods, and, in short, pay off in marketing and free advertising. Even if it only sold a few hundred, it would sell enough regular Dodges to pay for itself.

That said, Iacocca was counting pennies in product development, and his own 'TC by Maserati' project was failing. The idea was to have Maserati come out with its own car, new and snazzy; then, the Chrysler LeBaron could show up with 'Maserati-like' styling. The TC, though, was delayed by over a year; when it came out after the LeBaron, the auto press had a good laugh at its expense. The Viper would be different; Castaing and Lutz would have full control over the development process, and its success was already pretty well proven by the car-show reception.

Some talked about making the project cheaper by switching to a V8, even as the prototype was being created. At least one person thought of using a modified version of an experimental aluminum 426 Hemi V8 from the early 1970s. Team members even went to visit Keith Black, who made a highly reputable aluminum-block 426 Hemi (the phrase "Keith Black Hemi" was in nearly every issue of some magazines). There were problems with that idea, though; Hemi engines are notoriously wide, and using the 426 would have required fundamental changes to the Viper's shape. A smaller, twin-turbo or supercharged V8 would fit, but would not be consistent with the 'back to basics' theme.

Those discussions never went anywhere, partly because, as Iacocca reportedly said, a V8 Viper might be seen as little more than a copy of the Cobra or Corvette, and using the old 426 Hemi would send the wrong message to the magazines. It needed the V10 for image, and to be sure of clobbering well-modified AC Cobras.

The V10 may have made all the difference. Jim Julow, vice president of Dodge in 2002, reflected, "Back in 1992, the purpose was to re-orient what the Dodge brand was all about. We had just come out of a lot of years without any significant performance-oriented products. We needed to send a message that we had a new concept … something that was so outrageous, so cutting-edge, so purpose-built that it said we still had a lot of car nuts around here; people with the know-how to put the most outrageous street car ever on the road."

BACK TO THE FUTURE OF PRODUCT DEVELOPMENT

Around halfway through the project, top management had to greenlight it for production – or end development. Lee Iacocca was the key man, taking responsibility and authority for any such major decision.

The established story is that the leaders of the development team had Iacocca drive the car; and then he got out and said, "Get this thing built!" (Is the story literally true? Perhaps. However, it was also staged, on May 18, 1990, in front of auto reporters; he threw Lutz a set of keys, and yelled, "Build it!")

The "build it" story works, whether true or not, because of Iacocca's rapid-fire approach. He wanted a convertible, so planners and engineers rushed to get one, albeit flawed and expensive, into production; when it was an instant success, engineers made it better and cheaper. Lee demanded a luxury car, and the Executive, Limousine, and Imperial were born, struggled for a time, and dropped. Iacocca wanted a version of the Plymouth Voyager for higher-income people, and the Chrysler Town & Country was created; it outlasted the Plymouth Voyager.

Some of Iacocca's edicts were more successful than others, but he was making things happen in a company which, for decades, had been scared to try anything not already tested by Ford and General Motors. What's more, Iacocca's demands were not usually as whimsical as they seemed. Convertibles were a publicity item which other automakers had stopped making; and he figured any automaker needed to make luxury cars. The Town & Country was likely derived from a stray comment at the country club or a product planner, but, in retrospect, an obvious profit-maker.

The case for the Viper was strong, too. Auto writers and buyers had all but given up on Chrysler and its endless recycling of K-car technology. Rebates and discounts were growing rapidly as Chrysler, Plymouth, and Dodge cars were increasingly seen as dull and old-fashioned. Dodge could offer an Omni GLHS that whipped most (or all) of the old muscle cars on the track, or a Spirit R/T with the best acceleration you could get from a sedan in the United States; but they remained unseen by most buyers. 'Father Viper' himself, Roy Sjoberg, later pointed out, "Lee Iacocca was concerned that the only good press we had was a world-class cup-holder, and that was our K car."

There was also the internal, organizational aspect of the Viper. Chrysler Engineering had gone from leading the world to being slow and hidebound, not because the actual engineers or managers were slow or hidebound, but because the culture and structure got in their way. Developing the production Viper took less time and far less money than, say, creating the Dodge Shadow/ Plymouth Sundance, essentially by shortening the Dodge Spirit/Plymouth Acclaim and integrating parts of the Dodge Daytona suspension into it. Thus, the key words in Iacocca's speech at the 1992 Detroit Auto Show came at the end: "We want to show you what an American car company can do when we put our minds to it. In 1989, this Dodge Viper was just a concept. In January, it'll be rolling off an assembly line in Detroit, Michigan. Nobody in the country ever developed a car that fast."

He added, "We've changed this company to give you even higher-quality cars faster and at lower cost. For those of us who forgot, it's called being competitive."

More importantly, he told how Chrysler was assuring itself of a future: "From now on, every new car Chrysler makes is going to be built the way this one was, and that's by a team: product and manufacturing engineers, designers, finance guys, and marketers all working together with one idea, making a great car."

Iacocca was not announcing a new car, as much as he was describing Chrysler's new platform-team approach. In the past, Chrysler had used a slow and noncollaborative development process, so its new cars took a long time to get from idea to factory floor. Development was expensive, and the end result was usually not innovative – a real problem at a company once set apart for its engineering.

When Chrysler took over AMC, the smaller company's engineering chief, François Castaing, started pushing Iacocca to switch from function-based engineering to platform-based engineering. He wanted a single team to develop one or more cars on a common set of dimensions and basic architecture, so that the company would be organized not by function, but by carline – one team each for compact cars, midsize cars, large cars, minivans, trucks, full-size vans, each Jeep, and the Viper.

Chrysler had used a platform team before, to create the 1960 Valiant, a revolutionary car for the company; its development was an odd parallel for the new Viper. The Valiant rebuild Chrysler's presence in Europe, Australia, New Zealand, South America, and parts of Africa; but Chrysler had not used platform teams since the Valiant was launched.

Ironically, the original 1924 Chrysler had been built by the platform-team method, within Maxwell Motors. A small team of engineers had created the revolutionary car in an area set apart from the regular engineering organization.

In press releases, Chrysler said it was basically copying Honda; in reality, it was adapting AMC's engineering process to fit a much larger, more complicated company. The advantages of platform teams were speed, coordination, and cross-fertilization of ideas; the downside was that functional areas would not develop the depth of expertise they would need in the long run.

In any case, Iacocca credited the Viper as showing how Chrysler would be creating cars in the future; and Tom Gale called the Viper "a prototype for how we were going to manage the company, going forward." Gale called the Viper project "a wonderful experiment … the prototype for the way we later reorganized the company into platforms." Even the leader of the Viper team said: "The platform team approach was initiated with the LH [large car] program and Viper. We knew the Viper would come out first, so it was used as the development program. We kept in close ties on culture development."

THE DIRECTIVE AND THE CHANGES

One key goal was to beat the Shelby Cobra from zero to 100mph (161km/h) and back to zero – 15.0 seconds. That would be tough; the Cobra had been built in the days before modern safety or emissions rules, and the Viper was expected to beat that time with every run, every car, not just a well-tuned example. A less audacious demand was to 'be ethical and moral.'

Iacocca set down an edict that no one was to change any of the dimensions from the concept car. That edict was not as absolute as it sounded, because some changes were essential; for example, Warren Steele wrote, "When the Viper was tested, it turned out that the windshield was too low; the wind would blow off the driver's hat and hair! Adding three inches (around 76mm) to the windshield height and removing the integrated mirrors solved the problem and saved significant tooling dollars. Both revisions were approved at a Friday status meeting."

Another issue was mounting the headlights in the hood; the vibrations made that impractical, and Iacocca approved securing them to a radiator structure. Lee also violated his own rule about a year from launch, when he demanded it "put a top on my car!" That set the team to scrambling for a top and side curtains that could be stored in the trunk.

Somewhere along the way, Team Viper discovered that the right and left sides of the show car were slightly different, as well, which it had to resolve before production.

All through the process, Castaing, Lutz, Shelby, and Team Viper kept the car simple, eschewing basics (moving windows), popular options (air-conditioning), and advanced technology if they didn't fit the core mission. Quite aside from the purity of the concept, eliminating options and certain technologies made it possible to hit their time and money budgets.

Many in the team saw problems with using a V10, particularly weight distribution. Carroll Shelby pushed for a V8, because he valued low weight over higher power; and in any case, a V8 twin turbo engine could match the performance of the V10. Lutz and Iacocca argued that a V8 Viper would just be another hot rod; Lee Iacocca had the same answer when told that routing the exhaust pipes to the sides of the car was impossible, and they would need to have them routed at the rear, as usual. It would just be another hot rod if the exhaust didn't come out of the sides, he said.

Other problems included snaking a steering column down to the steering box and, for maintenance, reaching all the sparkplugs; but these issues could be resolved with time and creativity.

Roy Sjoberg at the 30th Team Viper reunion.
(Courtesy L Scott Swanson)

FINDING THE LEADER

Bob Lutz and François Castaing quickly found a project leader who might have been born for the role. In 1985, when Chrysler, Ford, and General Motors (GM) were exploring the use of composite materials, Chrysler had hired Roy Sjoberg away from GM to work on its 'Genesis car.' Roy's experience included work on the GM-Ford CAR project; he had also worked alongside Zora Arkus-Duntov, 'Father of the Corvette,' for three years as development manager of the storied sports car.

Roy wrote that, while he was being recruited by Chrysler, "my friend and boss Bob Stempel [then a GM vice president] allowed me freedom to negotiate. Chrysler Materials had a lot of problems, so Robert Sinclair [Chrysler's head of engineering, who retired in 1987] asked me to take it over. All I knew about materials was what I'd messed up in design projects, but I took the job and solved issues, especially an OSHA audit that would have closed our doors. It was not creativity, but 'benchmarking,' finding out what is working and what isn't, then developing the package that maximizes its performance. I showed Bob Sinclair how a matrixed platform concept could work."

He added, "Bob Steele was my secret mole while negotiating for the job at Chrysler. When I was asked how I knew so much about Chrysler administration, I freely told them about my stepbrother, but they never found a Bob Sjoberg! Until I introduced him to Bob Sinclair."

Roy Sjoberg was named Executive Engineer of the Viper project in February 1989, but Roy and Zora Arkus-Duntov lived just three doors apart, and they regularly met over Martinis. Roy wrote that after Zora sold his Corvette, "I actually drove him to the Million Corvette celebration in

a Chrysler minivan!" He dropped Zora off a block away, so people wouldn't see his ride.

Once the Viper program was approved, Roy Sjoberg was an obvious choice to run it. His experience in working around big-project rules at the notoriously bureaucratic General Motors would be handy at the smaller, but still bureaucratic, Chrysler Corporation, and he had experience with both composites and sports cars.

Castaing and Lutz asked if he wanted the weekend to think over the new job; and Roy said, "Hell no, that's just what I want to do." It was the ideal job for him, and he was ideal for the job. Not only did he have expertise in the materials and niche, but he knew how to get the most out of a team – and it was always about the team. For years after he retired, he admonished people writing about the car to "credit Team Viper."

The early Viper team with the V8 mule car; Roy Sjoberg
is hidden in the driver's seat.
(Courtesy FCA US; provided by Warren Steele)

GETTING THE MONEY AND THE PEOPLE

François Castaing had estimated the cost of the project at $70 million, and Roy Sjoberg estimated it at $60 million. Roy Sjoberg said that the Treasurer, Steve Miller, nixed those budgets. Iacocca had $100 million he could spend without challenges, but he had already spent half of it on the Town & Country minivan. That left $50 million, and Steve Miller reportedly said, "You're going to do it for $49.9 million. In a billion dollar corporation, that rounds out to zero, so no one will see you or hear you or know you exist … The day you spend that dollar over $49.9 million, call me."

Sjoberg would be in charge of the project, but Lutz, Gale and Castaing created the Viper Technical Policy Committee to make sure the project stayed on track, without getting in the way – to assure success without the constant meddling that slowed down many Chrysler projects.

As the first platform team of many, Team Viper would provide lessons for the Chrysler executives; and the experienced team of Lutz, Gale and Castaing (with Carroll Shelby as a consultant, when his health allowed it) could help Roy Sjoberg to lead his first full-production development project. Roy later said of the Jeep/Truck Engineering leader, "François and I did not always see eye to eye, but he supported the Team and provided his race experience and contacts."

The committee met weekly, and Sjoberg would bring up design questions for a rapid resolution. Carroll Shelby, who was having heart issues, was mainly an inspiration; he also pushed hard for weight reduction. He had often said that while you can add horsepower to overcome weight, it wouldn't help in the turns.

With a budget and structure, Roy Sjoberg had to recruit people – the kind of people who would be energized about a sports car, would understand the project principles and needs, and, perhaps, would stay around after work to keep things moving. They didn't have detailed, computerized human resources record at that point, so a quick database search was out.

Roy talked about it with Lydia Fleming, and they decided to ask anyone who might be interested to meet in the design studio's styling dome; they brought the concept car and Bob Lutz, Tom Gale, François Castaing, and Carroll Shelby. They invited around 60 people, according to Herb Helbig, and around 250 were there. Roy said, "I asked the fellow in the car to blip the accelerator … once he got the idea of hitting the accelerator in the styling dome, it made such a wonderful noise that we had a lot of volunteers interested." The idea was to find "the people that raced motorcycles, raced cars, had a love for high-performance and hotrods."

One of those people was Herb Helbig, transmission development supervisor and future head of Viper engineering development, who was to earn the nickname "the Grail-keeper." Herb first heard about the Viper show car on the radio; he went to the show and couldn't find the car, but then he noticed "a sea of people around one turntable." When he got to the front of the crowd, he saw "this unbelievably sexy, gorgeous, magnificent supercar called the Dodge Viper, and I was smitten with this thing. I thought to myself, being the cynical engineer that I was, 'No chance in the world they'll ever build this car, because they've tried to do stuff like this in the past but it never happened.'"

Show-goers almost all said the Viper was the best car there, and people had gone up to Bob Lutz and other Chrysler people, wanting to write checks to hold their spot on the waiting list. "People were saying, 'Don't care what it costs, I just want the car.'"

Herb called up Roy Sjoberg and asked for an interview, and Roy pointed out, "You understand that if we do this, you have to give up your job, and if the program goes up in smoke you don't have a job. You've got to go back and see if you can find a place to work." Herb said it "probably took me a nanosecond" to say yes.

There were risks to signing up. The program would not be approved for production until around 18 months into development, and Chrysler had its share of projects that

The Viper pace car at the Conner Avenue plant. (Courtesy Patrick Rall)

The pace car had switches for the sport-bar strobe lights under the climate control, which deceptively showed an air-conditioning label. The steering wheel already had a Viper logo. (Author)

went well and then disappeared. If that happened, the team members would have to hope they found another job in the company; their old job would not be waiting for them.

Another early team member was Dr Helen Cost, the lone interior person on the original team. She later said, "when Roy lit up the car and the sound of the mufflers went off in the Styling Dome, I said, 'I am doing this.'" After she joined the team, she made a timeline with various milestones she had to do – then went to Roy's office, found a massive time chart on the wall (with over 900 events), and tried to figure out how her work would fit into it.

Another early team member was Dara David; she interviewed with Herb, and thought the main reason she was able to join was that he saw spark in her eye "and the fact that I was drooling over this car." As she got to know the team, she came to the conclusion that they were all "seasoned racers, seasoned pros. They knew cars inside and out. They could build cars in their garages."

Roy Sjoberg had criteria for team members, even at suppliers: they had to love racing or performance cars, and know the cars. When he was lining up a supplier for interior pieces, he rejected the first team, and asked to walk around the facility. Then, in his words, "Saw a race helmet: 'I want that guy.' Went around, saw motorcycle racing pictures: 'I want that person.' We got three people

Dodge sold pace car special editions; there are few clear differences between this and the actual pace car. (Courtesy Marc Rozman)

who were really into performance, and when we talked about it, they understood what they had to do."

Roy Sjoberg did his best to avoid surprises from suppliers; he told an audience at Chrysler, "Go visit them, at weird hours. I was there at one in the morning, one time. If they know you care, they'll do something."

The project didn't always get cooperation, partly because it seemed like a long shot, and was running counter to the routine; but, as Roy Sjoberg wrote, "Lack of cooperation with small, out of the norm projects is normal at large companies. When we started, François Castaing tacitly supported us and let me deal with the naysayers. I knew how to do this."

One way to get cooperation was giving people rides in the new car, starting with the first mule car, VM01 (Viper Mule #1); it looked like the final car, other than lacking doors, a trunk, and the sport bar. Herb Helbig later said, "I was privileged to give a number of thrill rides in that car to skeptical executives inside the company … Many, many people inside the company had no idea about the joy of driving, the passion for the machinery, the one-to-one connection that goes on with guys and gals who love cars. They just didn't get it. I'd take them up on the oval at 140 miles an hour, no top on the car, wind in their hair, the wind screaming, the engine screaming, and they would get back and get out of the car and say things like, 'Now I understand completely why we must do this.'

"One person at a time, we changed the company over to be advocates. As we got closer and closer to production, we had more and more support inside the company. People wanted us to succeed because everybody realized that we were onto something big."

Roy had a graphics person as well, "because management can't read drawings," a lesson from Zora Arkus-Duntov. Zora also, incidentally, suggested calling Roy "Father Viper" because Zora himself was "Father Corvette." It worked out: "Father Viper was more applicable to being a priest over this wonderful group of people – a fantastic group of people."

When all else failed, Roy Sjoberg could appeal to Lee Iacocca. Roy referred to Lee as their hydrogen bomb, because "he was our mentor and the bureaucracy knew it. Whenever I got told 'You can't do that,' I'd say, 'That's fine, just write a note to Lee Iacocca and I'm sure he'll put us on the straight and narrow.'

"Lee never got a letter, because there was a secret method with Lee's secretary: when she got letters to Lee Iacocca, they were handled by her. But if she opened a letter to Lee Iacocca and there was another letter inside to Lee Iacocca, that went straight to Lee. That was our means of communicating."

It would be hard for the executives to stay completely out of the way, and one case, according to Carney's book, was the "sport bar" which went over the seatbacks. Sjoberg insisted on it for safety; though it wasn't a true rollover

bar, it would provide some protection in a rollover, and it helped to increase the body stiffness. Castaing didn't like it, and it was missing from the first prototype; but every other Viper prototype did, and it was on the production car. The bar added a little safety margin, made the car faster and cheaper to build, and likely helped cornering or weight loss.

The sport bar also helped Vipers to be parade cars: it was a place for VIPs to during a parade, so it had to support that weight, without adding too much to the car's own weight. Team members worked on it, but couldn't get it quite right; even Al Bederka, who had worked on the Corvette (which had a similar piece), had a hard time with it.

VM01 was built at a shop lent by Jeep, which the team called "the snake pit;" the white Viper was powered by a tuned, 300hp (224kW) iron-block 360 V8, which had around the same weight as the aluminum V10 would, so they could start to dial in the front suspension. The car five-speed gearbox was a placeholder; wheels came from Boyd Coddington's shop. Herb Helbig was the tire and wheel guy, and Dave Buchesky was the suspension engineer.

The car was ready; who would drive it first? It was a cold Saturday when some members of Team Viper took the prototype to the Proving Grounds, for the first time a Viper had ever really been driven. Jim Sayen recalled that Roy asked who would go first; Dave Bucheski volunteered, and Roy appointed Jim to be the passenger. When his turn to drive came, Jim said that Dick Winkles, his passenger, took out his computer and hooked it up to the car to check the engine readings. Sayen said, "I took off, got up to speed, went to make my first turn, completely lost it, and spun around in circles about three times. Dick was holding on, and when we came to a stop, he said, 'Well, you got that out of your system now?'"

The second prototype (VM02), built in 1990, used an iron-block V10 and a BorgWarner transmission; the body panels were fiberglass, painted red. Production cars at Chrysler had a two-letter code; the Viper's was SR, named for the Lockheed SR-71. Some of the codes had no deeper meaning, though some either were chosen as acronyms or turned into acronyms later. The Grand Wagoneer, a "Senior Jeep," was coded SJ; many claimed the "LH" large car (Intrepid, Concorde, Vision, LHS) stood for "Last Hope," though L may have only designated "Large." In any case, the Viper's SR code lasted until 2002; the 2003-2010 series were coded ZB, and the final series was coded VX.

THE SKUNKWORKS EFFECT
In the 1950s, Chrysler pulled a rabbit out of its hat with the original Valiant; the humble compact car rebuild sales in Europe, South America, and Australia, and some of its innovations spread to Chrysler's entire product range.

The secret behind the Valiant was its development by a small team, in a small space away from the headquarters complex.

Because the team was small, people from different functions worked in the same room, and the usual boundaries dropped away; doing your piece and tossing it over the wall to the next group was much harder when the next group sat next to you. Designers made things easier for the engineers, engineers made it easier for the production groups, and cross-pollination of ideas helped people to solve problems quickly and in novel ways. Innovative ideas were implemented quickly without "not invented here" barriers.

The Valiant team was also split from the main company; at the time, it was done because the Highland Park headquarters didn't have enough space. With the Viper team, it was deliberate.

These small teams are often called 'skunkworks,' after the Lockheed P-80 development team during World War II; the nickname came from being in a circus tent next to an odiferous plastic factory. Ben Rich's *Skunk Works* told the story of the Lockheed team that created the U-2, Stealth bomber, and SR-71 (hence the Viper's SR body code); another deep look at a skunkworks was Tracy Kidder's *The Soul of a New Machine*, which showed the creation of a new computer by a small group which beat a larger, better-funded team at the same company.

Sjoberg gave all 85 of the original Viper team members a copy of Ben Rich's *Skunk Works*, and later told Matthew Stone that there were five keys to Team Viper's teamwork: vision, product passion, being hands-on, empowerment and accepting risk, and management by coaching.

Skunkworks teams are small, protected from normal rules, and separated from mainstream groups. The Viper's special place was at the Jeep/Truck Engineering (JTE) facility on Plymouth Road, the Plymouth Road Office Complex. A grand building in a decayed neighborhood, "Plymouth Road" was built to make Kelvinator refrigerators; then Nash bought Kelvinator, Hudson merged with Nash to form AMC, and Chrysler bought AMC, bringing the Plymouth Road building into the fold.

Pete Gladysz, chassis manager, heard that Jeep's designers were moving from Plymouth Road to the main complex. That night, Roy Sjoberg confirmed the rumor and, helped by François Castaing, moved his team (then 26 people) into the space. He knew they had to get away from the bureaucracy.

When they arrived, they found two huge (and unused) freezers, which the Viper team stored its performance parts in. Roy Sjoberg recalled, "It was so deserted that when Ray Schilling opened the first deep freezer, [he found] a Nash Metropolitan, a World War II Jeep, and some other vehicles."

It was basically an empty space with no telephone lines or computers. Fortunately, Pete Gladysz related, a few of the Viper team had friends in the right places, and over the next weekend, the office equipment arrived. He also had a friend in the computer center; "he knew where there were a whole bunch of [graphic computers] sitting around going to dust, so the following weekend we moved a semi-truck in and cleaned out the warehouse."

Roy later clarified, "We 'confiscated' Chrysler computer graphics machines, as the system had been replaced by CATIA and all the equipment was in a warehouse, and trained everyone with a retired designer who had developed the system and was able to enhance it. Two years later, we were 'caught,' and the system was eliminated after we all trained in CATIA."

Team Viper's workspace was ideal because it was so far from Highland Park; it took a long time to drive there, and once you arrived, you had to walk for a while, so casual visits were less likely. Chrysler's media writers would later echo Valiant publicity materials, saying that the offices were specially chosen for secrecy (one press release called the Plymouth Road space a "highly secured area of a major corporate engineering center") – but we know the reality.

The room was well designed for a team; it was a large open space, rather than a nest of offices or cubicles. Roy recalled, "When we first got there, everybody had their desk facing the wall. But after about six weeks, all of a sudden, all the desks had turned around and people were looking at each other and conversing and understanding what the other person was doing."

As Sjoberg told *Motorweek* in 1992, "The conventional method of automotive industries and large organizations has been that you go from A to Z by going from point A to B to C to D. With simultaneous engineering, it's all happening at the same time, concurrently." This didn't happen right away for everyone; it was a culture change, and could be uncomfortable. But, in the end, "everyone makes their designs collaborative, so that the product is manufacturable at the same time it is being designed."

Herb Helbig also talked about the floor plan: "We had a single team room, which was kind of unique in those days. We had everybody that was involved in the program in one year including the mechanics, all the fabrication work, and a car lift all right next to where the engineers had their desks, so we were literally all in one room all together. We actually were the prototypes for the platform concept that Chrysler later adopted, and we were really the guys who brought the first car to market from the platform concept."

Sjoberg added another advantage to small quarters: "We would ring a bell to get everyone's attention. Once in a while, to get attention, I'd roll a practice hand grenade down and everybody knew something was wrong. By the way, I've given that grenade to the chief of police; I had to disarm it in front of them." (The bell had a legend taped onto it: "Ancient Viper bell – from Tibet, used by secret religious order to call snakes." Roy Sjoberg may not have the grenade, but he still has the bell, and used it at the 30th reunion for events and announcements.)

Herb Helbig added: "We basically had three levels of engineering. There was Roy, a management level, and then everybody else. When Roy needed a decision, he would ring that bell and bring everybody together and say, 'Okay, this is what we need to decide,' and we would decide it.

"This meant that we would make decisions that would apply to the car in a matter of minutes, as opposed to weeks and months on the bigger platforms that had many, many more people. This streamlined approach to engineering and production was what allowed us to get the car into production in such a short amount of time."

Putting people together helped them to learn about potential problems more quickly, too. In the context of talking about communication, benchmarking, and controlling interfaces – how people in different groups interact – he said, "I've never seen anyone shoot themselves in the foot, but man, can they kill people around them! Normally, it's because, 'Well I didn't think it mattered.' But when you're in a room together as a group they'd hear things. For example, one day, Bo [Dave Bucheski] was near Craig Belmonte; Bo had the chassis and Belmonte had the structure. One was saying something over the phone, but the other said 'I can't do that!' Communication is really important."

Working on this kind of project, in this way, gave people a chance to stretch their intellectual legs. Herb Helbig had specialized in transmissions; normally he'd find it hard to break out, but in Team Viper, he learned more and became responsible for subsystems that involved steering, suspension, axles, driveshaft, other drivetrain parts, and how to put the car together. This type of experience created a much more well-rounded engineer.

Experienced and novice engineers worked together, the latter bringing in some new ideas. Dara David, who worked on wheels, tires, steering, and some drivetrain components in the early days, said she was just out of the training program. "It was a big learning curve for me because a lot of this technology was new. A lot of the folks who were already there kind of helped me through that learning curve; it was just a matter of learning the systems and understanding them."

In a tightly knit group, people cared more about finding a solution than who proposed it; as Al Bederka said, "that could just as easily be the janitor standing next to the vehicle as it was us … It was amazing, sometimes, the logical solutions that came out of the mouths of people you never expected."

Roy Sjoberg nurtured Team Viper, personally paying for off-site celebrations to keep up the team's spirit and cohesiveness. When asked questions for this book, he consistently reminded me to credit Team Viper. It paid off with a team spirit that brought more out of people. One of the team's engineers, James Finck, said in 2017, "Viper team members are some of the hardest working and best engineers that I've ever worked with in my life. It was a real blessing to be part of something like that, that actually became a family."

Roy also knew it wasn't only about the people who went to work each day; their families had to support the project, given all the night and weekend work. "If the family was involved, they'd understand why their spouse

1989 Concept and 1994 production Viper at Eyes on Design 2018. (Courtesy Marc Rozman)

does this. They'd come to Chelsea and get a chance to drive the car or have picnics and activities, and they'd say, 'I understand. I may not like it all but I'll work through it.' … Our wives and family were really important, because without that support, you're empty."

The core group was hand-picked; Sjoberg started out by going to various engineering groups, and asking for one person from each to be transferred into his group. When he needed to, Roy also reached out to retirees – people from both Chrysler and GM's Corvette team. This included Larry Rathgeb and Ralph Youngdale, from Chrysler's racing group; Al Bederka, Andy Tevin, Dick LaPointe, and Roger Kykola from the Corvette team; and Willem Weertman, the legendary Chrysler engine designer who had a hand in every engine from the company's classic V8s to the current Hemi. Murray Bursott (hardware design), Andy Tevin, and Al Bederka had all been Marines during the Korean War.

HITTING THE TARGETS

The longer the Viper team could put off hitting $50 million, the longer they could work without interference. They tried to avoid buying computers, test rigs, and prototyping equipment; instead, they found tools or devices that weren't being used, and borrowed or traded for them.

There were times when it was easier to avoid questions. One of the early Team Viper people advised a co-worker to start driving a Dodge MaxiVan (a large commercial van), without a passenger seat; because, with the right windshield decal, he could go through security without being checked. Roy Sjoberg later told an audience of Chrysler employees, "If you were missing stuff, it all ended up over at Jeep Truck, in the Viper team center."

There were other ways of keeping costs low. Tooling for a legally-required side marker lamp would cost around $160,000, so they checked Chrysler's parts bins, then went rummaging at Murray's Auto Parts. They found a light that would work, and attached it to the clay model; designer Neil Walling reportedly saw it and said, "I like that change." Then Mike Cipponeri had to find the manufacturer. Fortunately, the rep was going to Detroit anyway, and brought some samples – but it was not legal; it was a trailer lamp, not a sidelight. The rep realized, though, that they could make a sidelamp version – for just $16,000 in tooling. That was 10% of the original estimate for a new sidelight.

The concept car's wraparound windshield included rear-view mirrors, but they blocked the side view out of the car, and in any case, would be far too expensive to tool. The designers found that Dodge Stealth mirrors would fit the Viper perfectly, slashing the cost.

Roy Sjoberg added that the door openers had been developed by GM for Buick, which had even tooled them – before deciding not to use them after all; so they were already available. The instrument panel controls "were

an upside down Ford system. The Viper was truly Johnny Cash's Cadillac song!" (The song, *One Piece at a Time*, told the story of a GM worker who, over 20 years, snuck out the parts to make a Cadillac – with a tailfin on just one side, dual headlights on one side and a single on the other, and so on.)

The engine computer was an incredibly unlikely but true story. There was no V10 engine controller yet, and the Lamborghini one they'd hoped to use was far too expensive. Dick Winkles ended up combining an existing four-cylinder and V6 computer, to get things working; but it worked well enough to last through the first two years of production, until the truck V10 controller was available.

Simple things like lenses, interior switchgear, parking brakes, and wheel hubs could be taken from the parts bins; but the Viper was mainly unique.

Adding to the mix was Chrysler's decision to move from its home-grown CADCAM software to Dassault's CATIA package, starting in 1989. CADCAM had been a major advance for the company, making design, engineering, and manufacturing more accurate and repeatable, with the ability to compute skewed views by machine. On one car launch (the Horizon-based Plymouth Scamp), Chrysler claimed its software increased productivity by a factor of three.

In the late 1980s, spurred by the AMC takeover, the company started comparing its CADCAM system with Ford's TBGS, GM's CGS systems, SDR, Pro Engineer, and others. Dassault's CATIA had greater precision (in simple terms, using more decimal places in positions and calculations) and the ability to take tooling wear into account when dealing with manufacturing projections (aided by the high precision). AMC already used CATIA, so they had in-house experts already. By the time Team Viper was gathering, Chrysler had started to move to CATIA.

The Viper team drew on people with CADCAM and CATIA backgrounds, as well as some who had no computer design experience at all. Brian Hoxie, who joined Team Viper in 1989, remembered, "Being a Chrysler employee, coming in from Highland Park, I had Chrysler CADCAM experience, and we also had people there in the Jeep/Truck building who had CATIA experience. We had people on the boards on Chrysler CADCAM, and people on CATIA, so it was an interesting operation in those days." Brian worked on parts of the body, and also acted as a Chrysler CADCAM facilitator.

Would the Viper be the first Chrysler car to be designed on CATIA? It did not have that honor; the 1994 Dodge Ram would be the first fully CATIA-engineered Chrysler vehicle. The Viper's body was designed on mylar, while the chassis was designed on CADCAM. In addition to being able to get the CADCAM computers relatively easily, the team included a retired designer who had helped to develop the system, and was able to enhance it. A couple of years later, the entire team was trained in CATIA, and the old Chrysler system was eliminated.

As the project continued, they started to bring people out of retirement to work on it, including Brian Hoxie's mentor, Ralph Youngdale. Brian asked Ralph about what he was doing in suspension geometry and layout; and the two worked together for over five years, with Brian learning about suspension layout and design. Being on Team Viper expanded the skills and range of quite a few people.

In all, the team had to create a brand new car, from head to toe, including the engine, in less than three years, while following Federal and company rules. The car was created with unprecedented speed, with a list price of $50,000 – half (or less) what people might pay elsewhere for similar performance. The designers and engineers needed to be fast, nimble, and focused, and to get unconventional ideas from any possible source.

The small team and fast timeline helped people with creative solutions; and Castaing, Lutz and Gale all looked to the Viper for new technologies. The Viper was the first Chrysler vehicle to have adjustable pedals, to make the car work with drivers of different heights, rather than having a great deal of seat back-and-forth movement; that ended up in trucks and minivans, and won an award from *Good Housekeeping*. Then there were the plastic body panels; once the panels were tried on the Viper, they could be applied to other relatively low-volume company cars (though, as it happens, they weren't).

THE BODY AND CHASSIS

When the Viper was conceived, Chrysler's sedans and coupes had all been unibody designs for decades; the company switched most of its cars to unibody in 1960. That wouldn't work for the Viper, with its massive power and limited price tag; instead, they used a tubular steel spaceframe, somewhat similar to the one used in the original Shelby Cobra and other contemporary racing cars, not to mention decades of Bristols. The Viper frame had a central structure with outriggers for the body panels, and provided an exceptional 5000lb-ft (around 6780Nm) per degree of torsional stiffness – just what you needed with 465lb-ft of torque (664Nm) coming on at low revs.

The Viper would use resin transfer molds (RTM) for the body panels. Glass fibers were placed within a mold, which was then closed so resin could be injected to mix with the fiberglass. The Corvette, in contrast, used stamped resin-impregnated glass mats.

In theory, RTM panels would be stronger and less-labor-intensive, with greater control over the finish. The main labor saving was in hand finishing – around 15 minutes per panel, versus hours for a stamped panel. RTM was cheaper than stamped fiberglass when producing fewer than 20,000 parts, and it resisted 'spider' cracking – which is why it was already used on cars such as the BMW Z1 and Lotus Elan.

The Viper used thinner body panels than the industry had used before – around 0.10in (2.5mm), versus around 0.125in (3.2mm) in other cars. Team Viper was the first to use RTM for the windshield frame, which had a foam-wrapped steel core inside an RTM outer surface – a one-piece design that also acted as the top of the instrument panel. The lower front of the body used fiberglass, and the clamshell hood was made from a sheet molding compound. The floorpan was molded sheet steel.

The plastic body panels took a long time to get right, and the formula wasn't quite working when production started; Bob Lutz pointed out that even his own car had sink marks in the hood and other flaws. The body panel fit was, to be gentle, not quite up to production-car standards. On the other hand, steel would never have worked for such low numbers; creating the durable stamping dies would have dramatically increased the cost of the car. The RTM panels would also provide some more flexibility in case of minor design changes, or additions such as the duct and fender louvers in the 1996 Coupe.

Aerodynamics was a major concern; the team had to balance reduced drag against keeping pressure on the tires (avoiding lift). They called in McLaren, which had a ground-moving wind tunnel, for help.

One of the challenges from the concept car was the side exhaust; the exhaust heat, amplified by catalytic converters, forced the team to switch from plastic to aluminum for the door sills. The side pipes were a burn hazard and, moreover, rather hard to engineer around; it was far easier to route the exhaust underneath and have it come out the back. It was no surprise, really, that there were no other production cars with side pipes – or that the production Viper would include a warning label for the door sills.

The heat of the engine, exhaust, and catalytic converter melted carpets and plastic door sills in the prototypes. Large doses of space-age insulation and this warning label resolved the issues.
(Courtesy Angela Puckett)

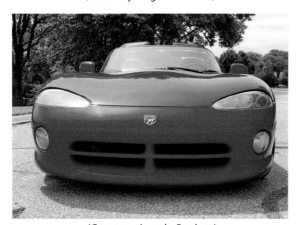

Under the hood of Angela's 1994 Viper. (Courtesy Angela Puckett)

(Courtesy Angela Puckett)

Viper Club of America Treasurer Angela Puckett's 1994 Dodge Viper RT/10 – looking good, a quarter of a century after its birth. (Courtesy Angela Puckett)

This first-generation Viper had no place for front license plates, which were required by some of the country's most populous states (California, New Jersey, and New York), not to mention Canada. Dodge later left a bracket in the trunk, but that still required owners or dealers to drill. The aftermarket came to the rescue; Viper PartsRack has sold thousands of front license plate holders that don't require any drilling, for every generation of the car.

SUSPENSION AND BRAKES

Forget beam axles and torsion bars; the Viper had an independent suspension using unequal-length upper and lower control arms in both front and rear. In back, engineers hooked up stabilizing toe links to the lower control arms. The shock absorbers and springs were Koni coil-overs, with a low pressure gas charge. Both front and rear had anti-roll bars. The suspension had quite a bit of travel – eight inches (203mm) worth.

Upper arms were made from tubular steel, while the lower control arms and the power-assisted rack and pinion steering were borrowed from the Dodge Dakota pickup. Those fearing the pickup parts may have hurt the Viper's steering can be comforted by knowing that *Road &*

Production Dodge Viper RT/10 at Eyes on Design 2018. (Courtesy Marc Rozman)

Track praised its "immediate and obedient" response and on-center feel.

The wheels were forged aluminum, with a 17in diameter; rear wheels were 13in (330mm) wide (at a time when a typical production car had 6.5in or 7in wide wheels), and shod in Michelin P335/35ZR-17 tires. The front wheels were narrower, at 10in (254mm), and were shod with P275/40ZR17 tires; the difference in width, which was to continue through the Viper's life, reflected the need for greater grip in back (V10 torque) and the need for steering feel in front. The tires were specially made for the Viper, and helped it to achieve 0.95g of lateral acceleration on the skidpad.

Creating the tires was a long process. Goodyear and Michelin were both called in to develop a tire for the Viper early in the process, since they had a V8-powered mule car early on. The companies each had a small team devoted to testing and modifying formulations and molds. Finally, in November, Team Viper chose Michelin as its sole supplier – over the objections of Purchasing, and even though the chairman of Goodyear had just made a huge donation to the Iacocca Research Center at Lehigh University. Lee Iacocca called Roy Sjoberg to confirm that the Michelins really were worth the trouble; Roy said they were, and Lee ended up saying, "I'll do the damage control."

The Chrysler and Michelin teams tested at the companies' tracks and at racing tracks; while they were testing the tires, other parts were breaking on these early prototypes. The exhaust heat melted the door sills and carpet; eventually, they used more and better insulation, and replaced the door sills with aluminum ones.

Working with prototypes was an adventure; the early models had no top, side windows, or windshield wipers. Wet-road testing used sprays which hit the hot door sills, presumably exploding in steam, and since there were no fender liners in VM01, the car stalled out when the water hit the computer. The driver had to wear a rainsuit.

At each test, Michelin brought a large number of tires, to be rated on numerous characteristics. Tires affect how it feels when you start turning, then when you keep turning, and then when you go straight again. They affect

*Vipers could set new records for grocery runs.
(Courtesy Angela Puckett)*

Top: Interior was similar to the concept.
Above left: Basic but informative gauges; the dark circle just above the steering wheel was a simple message center, including the brakelight and 'check engine' light.
Left: Gauge detail.
Above: Two large speakers were mounted between the driver and passenger seats. (All courtesy Angela Puckett)

launches, braking, and ride, and they do so differently in wet and dry, hot and cold. Fixing one problem causes others. The process required extensive driving on each set of tires, using a set course, then going back to the originals to make sure they remembered it correctly. It must have been exhausting but fun, driving the prototype Vipers as hard as close to the limits as they could, while trying to get repeatable results.

The brakes were an easier choice: 13in (330.5mm) vented discs for both front and back. In front, aluminum Brembo calipers had quadruple 42mm pistons; in back, they had single 38mm pistons. Antilock brakes were rejected due to time, cost, and purity, but the brakes did have power assist.

The power rack and pinion steering system had a 16.7:1 ratio, with just 2.4 steering wheel turns from lock to lock; the turning diameter, curb-to-curb, was 40.6ft (12.4m). Few reviewers noticed that the steering column came into the car at an angle, so the steering wheel wasn't straight; limited time and a massive engine brought compromises. Some did mention that the interior got rather hot, given less than ideal air distribution, the side pipes (and catalytic converters), and the engine placement. That would become a bigger issue, when the Viper went endurance racing.

Team members sometimes worked around the clock; as they got closer to production, they fine-tuned the chassis and powertrain at the Nelson Ledges and Road Atlanta tracks, using chassis prototypes (mules) first. Regardless of what some owners may think, they also did cold-weather testing, including a run up to Michigan's Upper Peninsula (Whitefish Point) for some cold-snow tests.

PROGRESS

The first mule, VM-01, had been finished in December 1989. Two months later, the second prototype (VM-02), with the sport bar and a V10, was built – and the company took an unprecedented step, inviting journalists to talk to the engineering team and take a ride with Bob Lutz at the wheel. *Automobile*'s creator, David E Davis, was given the first ride; the plastic door sills were smoking when they got back to the pit, and Roy Sjoberg doused them with water from the refreshments table.

At one point, according to the fable, Lee Iacocca test drove the car and demanded that the engineers add a soft top. The team came up with a canvas soft top and zipper-operated vinyl side windows for bad weather; and, eventually, a fiberglass roof, though early buyers wouldn't have that option. More to the point, Iacocca reportedly turned to Bob Lutz and said, "What are you waiting for?" That was allegedly the true green light for production.

Roy's story was a little different. The first time he took Lee Iacocca for a drive in a Viper, they started in the executive garage, just the two of them. Lee turned to Roy and said, "Now, Roy, they probably told you I don't know

how to drive a manual transmission." Roy wasn't sure what would happen next; but Lee laid rubber in the executive garage and said, "Do you believe me now?"

They went out, Lee driving, his trademark cigar in his mouth, and blew by a radar trap. The officer saw a vehicle he'd never seen before, coming out of the Chrysler engineering center, driven by somebody with a big stogey in his mouth. The officer didn't bother them.

When they returned, Lee commented, "Roy, that's a very small ash tray in this car." Roy told him it was from the rear door of the K-car, and Lee answered back, "Don't let anyone change that ash tray. That's terrific."

The Viper now stood at 3100lb (1361kg) – around 300lb (136kg) over its goal of 2800lb (1270kg). The team was benchmarking against other cars, some purchased, some borrowed; there was a Porsche 928, Mazda RX-7, original Cobra, Nissan 300ZX, and a Corvette, among others.

THE VIPER'S CHICKEN TEST

At Lockheed, when the company had a jet engine nearly ready for production, they would toss a raw supermarket chicken into the engine. If that destroyed the engine, the project failed, because they didn't want to have a planeload of people crashing every time a bird crossed the jet's path.

Sjoberg said, "The ultimate chicken test was Bob Lutz. We took Lutz for a ride [in prototype VM01]; the only real mistake we made was everybody looked at it and said, 'Well, damn, you're done.' It didn't have doors and it didn't have a hood, and it had a V8 engine we'd kind of pumped up, but it showed the principle."

Perhaps a more serious – at least a more public – chicken test was the 1991 Indy 500. Chrysler had won the pace car rights, and was going to use the Dodge Stealth, a sophisticated all-wheel-drive car with a 320hp (239kW) twin-turbo V6. The Stealth, though, was a Mitsubishi, built and engineered in Japan. The UAW was especially incensed at the idea of a Japanese car representing Chrysler at Indy, which had only used American pace cars.

The Stealth was an odd choice, since Chrysler had just launched the 224hp (167kW) Dodge Spirit R/T, which had a 141mph (227km/h) top speed and ran the quarter mile in 14.5sec – good numbers for 1991. If they didn't want to use a four-door, five-passenger sedan, they could have substituted the Dodge Daytona, with its Chrysler-engineered intercooled-turbo 2.2L four-cylinder rated at 174hp (130kW), could have easily done the job, based on some of the pace cars used in later years. Perhaps someone at Chrysler wanted to convince the Indy people to allow a Viper prototype?

Even given approval by the Indy 500 leaders, there were no actual Vipers available yet, and they would need two identical cars – a pace car and a backup. Team Viper met the challenge, providing the required two cars.

The celebrity pace-car driver, Carroll Shelby, had gotten a heart transplant nine months earlier; and the prototypes were fairly shaky at that point. When giving thrill rides, Shelby reportedly started holding his chest and feigning a heart attack, shaking a little bottle of pills. It scared quite a few people – but he was just joking, having a great time driving around the Speedway at 130mph (210km/h), with one reporter or dignitary after another in the passenger seat. He reportedly put in 1800 miles (2900km) without any problems.

The race winner was presented with a Dodge Stealth, since the prototype Viper wasn't street-legal. Roy Sjoberg said the winner objected: "I don't want a Japanese car. I want the Viper!" Once production started, he got his wish. Dara David remembered, "People were swarming around this car. Everybody wanted to drive this car. Carroll Shelby drove laps in it; then, afterwards, he taught me how to make chilli."

GETTING REAL

Lee Iacocca greenlighted the Viper production car and freed the rest of the funds for development. Now Team Viper knew it was real, and there was a new job: they needed to figure out how to build it, working with the plant to develop an assembly plan and technique that had not been done at Chrysler since the days of Maxwell Motors.

Herb Helbig remembered, "We were developing new body technology because the car had a plastic body. Oh, by the way, we had a brand new engine that we had to develop from the ground up, because we had the V10 truck engine, which was all cast iron, weighed 800 pounds and you couldn't put that in a sports car and expect any kind of performance out of it.

"If I knew how big a job it was going to be, there would've been more than just me freaking about how to do the whole works. But we decided early on that this was not going to be a feasibility study. Everybody in the engineering team room was committed to putting this car in production, even though a number of senior management considered it a feasibility study to decide whether we could really build it. We never considered it a feasibility study. We thought, 'We've got to figure out how to do this car because the company can't afford not to do a car like this.'"

Likewise, Al Bederka said, "The challenges in the beginning were simply, how the hell do you make room for the components they wanted to put in the vehicle that don't fit? … How the hell do we build the car? I went home and I woke up in the middle of the night one night, yelling at my wife that I know how to do it. And when I told Roy that I knew how to do it, he wanted to know how I could do that, and I told him 'Roy, you don't want to know,' and I didn't tell him."

The solution was to shove the engine over, past the steering, move the seats upward, reduce the sill, and move the steering column. Al Bederka continued, "Styling didn't find out about that until we had the first running car; then they told me, 'You can't do that.'" But it was done; Team Viper had overcome the challenges, solving them on the run.

The huge V10 also didn't leave any space for the usual windshield wiper mechanism, a surprisingly large assembly. The solution was using two minivan rear wiper motors, one for each blade; they had to be sealed against water, and computer-controlled to make sure the blades would never crash together. It was a clever solution, and may even have been cheaper than a mechanical setup.

In the end, with its massive engine, sturdy transmission, and roadster design, conforming to safety standards, the Viper weighed in 3476lb (1488kg). At least, that's a reasonable curb weight figure; in 1992, Car & Driver cited 3450lb, and the first press release declared "under 3400." In 2019, Wikipedia declared it to be 3284lb, without a source.

The 1992 price was right at the targeted $50,000, though buyers often paid far more due to dealer profit-taking. The passive seatbelts took the place of a driver's-side airbag, by US law; but even the 'passive restraints' required occupants to fasten a buckle. The lights conformed to United States, Canadian, and European standards.

The hood was a single piece of sheet-molded composite, hinged at the cowl – a 'clamshell' design. There were no exterior door handles, to save money; it was a roadster, after all. Federal law required door locks, so it had them.

A sticker on each door opening, readable when the door was open, warned occupants of the hot exhaust pipes, despite the Nomex heat barrier. Staying away from the exhaust pipes and door sill was, to say the least, prudent.

The seats had lumbar support, with adjustments for fore-aft movement and the angle of the seatback; instead of providing vertical adjustment, the Viper had power-movable pedals. The pedals had to be mounted further to the left than was desirable, because the engine took up some of the center space. There was no room for a "dead pedal."

Gauges were a compromise; the primary instrument cluster had a tachometer and 180mph speedometer, with warning lamps in a round pod. More information was shown on a series of gauges in the middle of the dashboard: oil pressure, fuel level, voltage, and coolant temperature. Gauges were light gray, with black pointers, backlit at night in amber and red.

Controls were basic, with an American-style headlamp switch, dials for heat, vent, and fan, and a toggle for the fog lamps. The parking brake lever was borrowed from the Chrysler LeBaron Convertible. The trim was cut from structural urethane foam trim, which had a crackle finish, and looked like ordinary plastic; it was the first use of that material as trim on an American-made car.

The Alpine stereo was decent enough, with six speakers, a cassette deck, and enough power to be heard over the wind and ten cylinders; the interior was largely dark, but the shift knob, brake lever, and parts of the steering wheel were done up in body-color.

The Viper, a fully-functional, regulation-conforming vehicle, had been developed in just 33 months. Cost-increasing features left out, but some weight-reducing and performance-enhancing changes couldn't be done, either, as systems and components were 'locked down' for production. The total cost was $50 million for parts and $35 million for R&D (François Castaing 'ate' the engineering overhead); along the way, Chrysler learned about independent rear suspensions, working with fiberglass and other plastics, and, most importantly, tested the platform team method.

The result may have felt crude; it may have seemed (as many said) like a kit car. It still had unique proportions,

Viper Coupe clay model as shown in the 1996 Viper GTS press book. (Courtesy FCA US)

Artist's rendering of the GTS. (Courtesy FCA US)

a thrilling look, and absurd torque; the performance was there, though the switch from absolute control to facing the wrong way from the bottom of a ditch could be rather sudden. It was about as far from a Chrysler Executive or Dodge Diplomat as anyone could get, because Bob Lutz, Tom Gale, François Castaing, and Roy Sjoberg had pushed aside all the normal compromises.

As Dara David said, one of the things that made the Viper unique was being hand-crafted, "engineered by a small group of people, with a limited (almost no budget), in a very short period of time; they brought it to market, and it became a phenomenon. It's now an icon. Even today, with more bells and whistles and windows and a roof that won't leak, it's still that hand-crafted car."

A car going through the normal channels could never have had the primitive soft top, the imperfect plastic panels, or the Viper's character. The team exercised a great deal of ingenuity in making the Viper conform to the budget and legal standards, and a great deal of discipline in sticking to the essentials. It was able to make something that people would love or hate (usually love), but that was definitely not aimed at 80% of buyers, or even 20% of buyers.

It's worth looking at some past Chrysler successes to see how much Team Viper accomplished, not just with the launch, but in succeeding years – how well they defended the Viper. The original Plymouth Fury was a performance-focused muscle car, but before long, the name was used for a full range of cars with economy engines. The Plymouth Road Runner started out as a low-budget, high-performance V8 car, with its own hot cam, bare floors, and the least of ornamentation; it ended up as just another trim level. The Dodge Challenger name went from a muscle car to a Mitsubishi four-cylinder. Even the Dodge Charger Daytona, a 200mph supercar, found its name on a rebadged Chrysler Cordoba after a few years.

The fact that the first car was relatively crude and focused on performance to the exclusion of nearly everything else had its own effect. Had the team been able to make it more appealing to a wider group of drivers from the start, they may have been restricted by reducing its appeal in later years. There was always pressure to save money and widen the appeal, say, through an automatic transmission and smaller engine. But the first Viper defined the line-up; it was not cuddly, accessible, luxurious, cute, or aimed at Joe Everydriver.

LAUNCH AND RECEPTION

The introduction of the production Dodge Viper to the media was part of a two-day event; on Friday night, the company invited a variety of famous racers, Jay Leno, and a group of reporters to a party. On Saturday, journalists drove the car on the street – a 300-mile route that included freeways, twisting mountain roads, and open desert runs; on Sunday, they hit the Willow Springs track. Team Viper

engineers checked reported issues on the prototypes in the middle of the Saturday trip. Carroll Shelby gave rides to journalists to show what a true race car driver could do with the power and traction. Media reviews were published in fall, long before the official auto-show launch.

It was a hard car to drive for the first time, between the grip and the clutching required to control 450lb-ft (664Nm) of torque. The rear could quickly slide out of control despite the 50/50 weight distribution. Most of the reporters were careful and respectful of the power; but most also put their foot down in the straights, and got an instant reward. The torque of the V10 was good for a sudden head-snapping acceleration, even from low revs.

The Viper team had beaten the old Cobra by a good margin; they reported a zero-to-100-mph-to-zero time of 14.5 seconds, shaving half a second off the Cobra's claim (an official USAC run was clocked at 14.78 seconds in 1993). It had a top speed of 165mph (266km/h) and generated 1G of lateral force in a 300ft (91m) circle. It had been a tough project; as Team Viper's Herb Helbig said, "We had to turn a fairy tale into real life."

The name was lengthened before release, since the team was already thinking about a coupe version; late weight-saving or performance ideas could be used in this new generation. The original Viper, then, was given a second name, in the spirit of the traditional Dodge performance moniker. Past muscle cars had been dubbed 'R/T', defined as either 'Rapid Transit' or as 'Road/Track;' put R/T with the number of pistons, move the slash, and you had the Dodge Viper RT/10. (You could also claim that RT stood for RoadsTer, but that seems unlikely.)

The public saw the Dodge Viper RT/10 in January 1992 at the North American International Auto Show in Detroit's Cobo Hall. By then, production cars were running off the line at the New Mack Avenue plant. In his keynote address to the world press, Lee Iacocca said, "VIN #1 is mine – and to hell with the rest of you!"

The reaction was impressive. Few thought Chrysler would do it; fewer thought they could do it. Many people assumed that the production car would be very different in powertrain and appearance, like the 1999 Charger concept and 2004 Charger sedan. Companies usually watered down concepts when they hit financial and production reality; that huge V10 was impractical, for a start; it would surely end up with a turbo-four, like the one in the Spirit R/T.

When Dodge released the Viper to a stunned world, they didn't just grab headlines and magazine covers; they readied car buyers for generations of Chrysler products that had fewer compromises than stretched, slammed, and lifted K-cars. Everything was different – and Chrysler would follow up its first act with ever-more-refined, ever-more-powerful Vipers and clean-sheet-design sedans and coupes.

Road & Track's Ron Sessions wrote about how the Viper turned heads in street traffic – and how many Los Angeles residents recognized it as it went by. He pointed out that it was wider (75.7in, or 1.9m) than the Corvette ZR-1 or Ferrari 348; it was also lower than the Ferrari F40 and Acura NSX, with a mere 44in (1.1m) of height. The body was incredibly rigid, despite the roadster form.

Sessions praised the shifter's "easy-to-find, precise gates" for their ease on track and in town, while noting relatively long throws. He described the "prodigious torque" and wrote about the 1500-5500rpm torque plateau, partly caused by the tuned intake runners.

Car & Driver attained a 13.2 second quarter mile time, beating the new Corvette ZR-1; the magazine's Kevin Smith pointed out that all the minor inconveniences disappeared in light of the insane torque and cornering. This was no muscle car that could go fast only in straight lines; it was a true track car.

Both Sessions and Smith agreed that it was easier to get into a Viper than a Corvette. Smith did not think much of the instrument panel material, but the controls were welcoming and familiar. He pointed out the problem with having the pedals pushed over to the left, including reaching for the clutch and finding the brake. He, too, did not think much of the V10's unique exhaust sound: "the Viper sounds oddly like a UPS truck up to 3000rpm, then it just roars like God's own Dustbuster."

While the clutch was heavy, Smith found it to be smooth, and, like Sessions, he found the shifter to be easy to operate. The engine was predictable, steering effort was light, and, in general, the Viper was easy to drive in traffic. The close and low windshield frame was a problem for visibility, while the sport bar hurt the rear view. Hard bumps could push the Viper off course, whether going straight or in a turn; but normally, Smith wrote, it was predictable and secure, with a little understeer and "minimal harshness." He also praised the structural rigidity. Still, the power and grip brought high speeds without apparent effort, which could mean rather severe consequences for miscalculations.

Both writers pointed out that Chrysler had not been known for passionate cars or hitting any extremes for quite some time. In this case, they had a car that outraced the Ferrari F355, Acura NSX-T, and Lotus Esprit S4S from 0-60mph, from 0-100mph, and in the quarter mile; cost at least $24,000 less than any of them; and could still take turns quite well (figures from *Car & Driver*).

Several writers commented on the Viper's feel, calling it a thinly disguised racing car; and Emerson Fittipaldi, two-time Formula One champion, said, "Driving the Viper is as close as you can get to driving a race car on the street."

Later writers called the car "twitchy" due to its short wheelbase (96.2in, or 2.44m) and stiff springs; pointed out that the side exhausts could burn the owners or passengers; and complained about the $1700 gas-guzzler tax, the result of a fuel economy rated at 13mpg city, 22 highway, according to the EPA, in 1992. That equates to around 5.5/8.9km/L, or 11 and 18L/100km; the actual 'numbers for comparison' to European standards would be different due to varying test methods. The 1999 Viper, as sold in the UK, was officially rated at rather pessimistic 20L/100km (combined/weighted) – 33.1L/100km urban,

2014 Viper gathering. (Courtesy Marc Rozman)

12.7 extra-urban. By then, US ratings had fallen to 11mpg (20L/100km) city, 20mpg highway (12L/100km).

One owner pointed out that the early cars were essentially hand-built exotics with "zero creature comforts, no air-conditioning, no cruise control. They were very hot inside, with the side pipes and headers; the manifolds and cats are on one side of you, and the manifold's in front of your feet. There were lots of air leaks and water leaks; most Viper guys didn't intend to drive it in the rain, so they didn't know it leaked like a sieve. Those of us who drove them regularly had to come up with techniques to stop leaks, without devaluing the car. Silicon sealer became our best friend, because it can peel right off after doing its job."

Another issue was getting the car aligned so it wouldn't follow every rut or seam in the road. Generally, in this generation, a decent number of people seemed to crash their Vipers in their first few months; Jon Brobst speculated that owners were careful with them at first, then drove faster and faster and faster; "Their skills didn't go up with their speed, so a lot of early Vipers were crashed." There was no stability control or antilock brake coming to the rescue; as Jon (and many other owners) said, "The only software to control the car is between the driver's ears."

Many of the most fondly-remembered cars were flawed; observers may wonder why people loved them so much, when higher-performing, more comfortable cars were made later (or even at the same time). Maurice Liang, who wrote several books about the Viper, said his favorite was still the original roadster; "I love driving that car. It puts a smile on my face every time … The suspension was tuned to be very neutral, so you can rotate the car in corners with subtle inputs from your right foot (though that is exactly why a lot of people don't like it, because you can spin it if you don't know what you're doing), and it has mountains of torque starting at low RPMs, whereas in the later cars, you have to rev the engine on takeoff.

"Add the wind in your face and the exhaust sound, and it's just a raw, visceral experience that few other cars can match. The Generation V ACR is clearly a superior car,

and I would definitely prefer it on the track, but for pure backroad fun on a sunny day, the RT/10 wins hands down."

The Viper team was also closer to owners than any other group at Chrysler; owners could call them directly to ask questions, and they met each other at annual events. Team Viper's James Finck said, "The appreciation they had for us, the people who designed and built the car, was just unbelievable … for someone to love that car as much as we do and just enjoy it on the track as much as on the road, was probably the most rewarding time that I've ever had working for a car company."

Even before starting work on the next generation, Roy Sjoberg tried to "continue the celebration," and kept the team creatively working together; he said, at the time, "As a team, we get together in November in the Moose Preserve and tell lies and show videos, and then we try to get together in the summer up at our place [his cabin in northern Michigan]. But camaraderie is really important and fun."

Team Viper was both improving the original and developing a coupe now. Some members of Team Viper were also kept busy getting parts for company Vipers as they were tested at the proving grounds or lent to journalists and executives. Someone on Team Viper might have to run down to the assembly plant on the far outskirts of Detroit to get parts. Team Viper's Fred Krupic remembered going to the plant for parts when it was closed; he'd take a tire along with him so he could tell Security, "I have to drop this off for production in the morning." Then he had to search the line and get the parts he needed – lifting, say, a differential, by himself – and take them back in the van.

Chrysler reported building 310 Dodge Vipers in 1992, which included some '93s. All 285 of the 1992 model-year cars had red bodies and a gray/black interior; black paint arrived with the 1993s. The first full model-year, 1993, saw production of 1043, only 50 of which were in black. Tom Gale got car 0001, and Jay Leno got an early black car. A single three-spoke 17in aluminum alloy wheel design carried all the 1992-1995 Vipers.

Jon Brobst picking up the first production Viper Coupe from the factory, with his Dodge 'Indy Ram.'
(Courtesy Maurice Liang)

Meanwhile, another new car was getting under way: the Plymouth Prowler. Tom Gale wanted an image-leader car for each brand, and Plymouth was next in line – before Chrysler. Gale saw a series of practical, retro-stylish Plymouths in the future, but Plymouth was shut down prematurely, and only the mass-production car in that line appeared: the PT Cruiser, which was assigned to Chrysler instead. (It was said that 'PT' stood for 'Plymouth Truck.')

One company engineer said the Prowler's main purpose, aside from its role as the Plymouth flagship, was to give Chrysler experience and expertise in lightweight materials. The Prowler used a great deal of aluminum, and had some industry firsts – all-aluminum seat structures and magnesium instrument panel cross-car structures (the latter would eventually reach the Viper). James Finck, for one, was on Team Viper, then the Prowler team, then, after gaining more expertise in lightweight materials, back on Team Viper. The Prowler may not have rebuilt Plymouth, but it did help Team Viper to learn more weight reduction techniques. Sadly for Chrysler, many of the Prowler team members were hired away by Ford in 1998-99 – which resulted in the Ford GT and aluminum-bodied Ford F-150.

Back at Team Viper, the 1994 model-year brought four available colors (red, black, Emerald Green, and Dandelion Yellow), a transmission reverse lockout, and amplified radio antenna integrated into the windshield. For the first time, a second interior style was available (black and tan, delayed from the 1993s), but only with Emerald Green paint. (The next color, white, was added for the 1996 cars.) Perhaps more important, at long last, buyers could buy air-conditioning for an extra $1200.

Was air-conditioning a betrayal of the 'back to basics' design, or a belated recognition that Dodge was convection-cooking its drivers? Neither: Roy Sjoberg wrote in 2019 that air-conditioning was always planned for 1994, but they had to find the right engineer, who turned out to be Ralph Molinaro. The system used R-134a refrigerant, which was still new.

The list price was now $54,500; 1994 model-year production reached 3083 – higher than Carroll Shelby's personal assessment of the market for all Vipers, over all time. It would be the most popular model-year for the Viper.

As the coupe drew near and the Viper continued to sell, there was pressure for automatic transmissions, traction control, and antilock brakes. Herb Helbig drew a line in the sand, and quickly earned the nickname 'Grailkeeper,' which he keeps to this day. In some cases, it was easier to convince others to keep with basics; for example, an automatic would have meant changing much of the frame. He eventually gave in on antilock brakes for safety reasons, but kept cup-holders at bay.

1995 Viper buyers got a passenger assist handle, storage pockets in the seat cushions, and a price boost to $56,000. Production fell to 1418; perhaps customers were getting bored? Perhaps not; Chrysler wanted to use New Mack to make truck engines. The Viper would be moved to its own factory, not far away from New Mack – a former sparkplug factory. The 345,000 square foot facility would be the Viper's home until the end; more immediately, in October 1995, it started producing the new 1996 Viper GTS Coupe. The sales drop was most likely due both to the factory move and rumors of the coupe.

PLANNING A COUPE

Team Viper knew, as the '92s rolled off the line, that they could do better with more time. They also knew that the Viper would have higher performance in coupe form because they could tune the aerodynamics more effectively.

The coupe marked a turning point for the Viper; it was no longer a one-off. The original plan reportedly had the Viper roadster in production until 1997, at which point it would be replaced by the Plymouth Prowler, which would in turn be replaced by a Chrysler flagship (say, the Atlantic), to surprise and delight buyers and the auto press.

The roadster was selling better than many had predicted, even with dealer markups; either the market had grown, or the Viper had fewer trade-offs than the 1970s sports cars. What's more, being on the Viper team was now a serious ambition for many or most of the employees; and Chrysler had gone full-bore into the platform-team concept. As work methods and the culture were changing, the company as a whole was getting more flexible, and there was more funding and better receptions at suppliers.

Tom Gale surreptitiously led the design team's work on the coupe, dubbed Viper GTS, reportedly finding new and different ways to hide the expenses; the car was developed at the same shop that had created the original.

A personal relationship helped shape the look of the new car: Bob Hubbach, lead designer of the GTS, was friendly with Peter Brock, who had created the Shelby Cobra Daytona Coupe – six cars specially built for racing. Brock supported the homage, which included a similar blue-and-white paint-and-stripe scheme and 'roof bubbles' so drivers could wear helmets.

Chrysler never kept the relationship a secret. Page six of the press release read, "Strongly evocative of the greatest GT cars, particularly the 1965 World Championship-winning Daytona Cobra coupes, the Viper GTS's functional, race-inspired details – the polished alloy quick-release fuel filler, twin helmet blisters in the roofline, and NACA-ducted hood – draw the eye further into the athletic bodywork while echoing its spiritual forebears." (A NACA duct is a low-drag air inlet on the hood, originally created by NASA's predecessor, the National Advisory Committee for Aeronautics, or NACA. The hood also had two air louvers just under the windshield).

Gale said he could count on selling a coupe to most of the roadster buyers. Many other people wanted a Viper, but didn't like the open-air driving, or the Viper's leaky, manually-installed top and vinyl side windows. With a permanently installed roof, people could enjoy the induction roar of the big V10 without having it drowned out by the scream of the wind.

The concept coupe was ready for the 1993 North American International Auto Show in Detroit just one year after the production RT/10 and four years after the original concept car. The blue-with-white-stripes Viper was shown with a matching aluminum V10-powered Dodge Ram, which eventually reached production as the Dodge Ram SRT-10.

The Viper GTS was the hit of the show. The main outward differences between the concept and production cars were the pillars, front fascia, and door handles; inside, one could find a spare tire and blackface gauges (the car had a black dash and lighter center console, whose color ran under the dash and onto the doors). Under the new skin was an RT/10 chassis.

The coupe gave new life to the roadster, because any updates for the coupe could be applied to the roadster as well. The coupe had luxuries like outside door handles and glass windows; real-life crash data showed how to take 140lb (63.5kg) from the body, while still passing government tests. Some weight was added back in with the comfort features, but the GTS was still lighter than the RT/10.

A stunning 90% of the RT/10's parts were changed to make the GTS. Part of that change was likely due to the switch to Dassault CATIA software, while the original RT/10 was designed on mylar and in Chrysler's old in-house computer-aided design (CAD) system.

The engine was redesigned, dropping 80lb (36kg) while adding power, ending up at 450hp (335kW) and 490lb-ft (664Nm) of torque. Part of that was due to the reworked cooling system, which let the engineers increase compression; as a result, owners had to move from midgrade to premium fuel.

Between lower weight and the updated engine, the coupe dropped 0-60mph times to 4.1 seconds (from 4.5) and provided 12.2-second quarter miles, ending at 118.8mph (192km/h).

Chrysler had been the first company to use computers in the automotive engineering process, and had created telemetry systems for the moon rockets and its own M-1 tanks. It should be no surprise, then, that once the car's design was in CATIA, computer modeling was applied to the frame and ended up increasing the already-fine torsional rigidity by 25%, and the beam strength by 12%.

Fortified by a milled steel top and an aluminum-alloy plate, the lightweight but rigid frame was 60lb (27kg) lighter than the original; Team Viper optimized the steel tubing diameter and wall thickness and stiffened the

2014 Viper gathering.
(Courtesy Marc Rozman)

joints, cutting weight while increasing strength. With track experience under its belt, the team also reinforced the differential mounts to make the car more stable under full throttle. The frame had a static torsional rating of 7600lb-ft (10,304Nm) per degree in the GTS.

In the 1996-99 Vipers (made before March 1, 1999), particularly aggressive driving could lead to cracks in the steering gear crossmember or differential mount. That led to Recall 998 and 999, in which dealers were told to inspect the crossmember and bracket, and replace any cracked parts; in addition, to prevent new problems, frame gussets and reinforcement brackets were installed. The parts packs included dozens of rivets and various reinforcements. The job involved grinding off old welds and making new ones, and took over five hours if no cracks were found. (These problems generally only came up when cars were raced hard at the track.)

The team also dropped around 60lb (27kg) of unsprung weight by switching to cast aluminum steering knuckles and control arms; it was also able to loosen up the shocks, helping to smooth out the ride a bit and handle rough roads better. To improve braking, engineers moved the lower ball joint to the control arm. Finally, the shock absorber mounts were moved further out on the control arms, which let the shocks travel more.

The original 50/50 weight ratio was a 46/54 ratio in the coupe; the GTS had both weight cuts up front, and a heavy glass rear window in back. The rear suspension had to be retuned because of the new weight ratio, but, with more track time under their belts, suspension engineers were more ambitious than that: they also moved the mounts to lower the roll center, and changed the rear caster angle from $-6°$ to $+1°$ for better stability in a straight line. This helped reduce the Viper's reputation for being somewhat treacherous in inexpert hands.

Changes cause more changes. Rerouting the exhaust meant that new heat shields were needed, and the weight, aerodynamics, and suspension changes required new tires. While the Michelin XGTZ had been ideal for the original Viper, the coupe had changed the equation; tire technology had moved on, and customers wanted better wet-weather traction. Besides, the tires were part of the plan to make the Viper more controllable for more people. They still had 17in wheels, though not for long.

TECHNOLOGY AND SAFETY

Once again, the Michelin and Viper teams worked together; Michelin making suggestions on suspension tuning, while Team Viper made suggestions on tires. Both had to balance the needs of the roadster and coupe; the latter pushed down more weight onto the wheels for high-speed traction. The teams also wanted to keep understeer steady near the limits of adhesion, making the Viper's handling at its limits more predictable and hopefully preventing some crashes.

Viper GTS in pace car trim. (Courtesy Marc Rozman)

Changes the team had run out of time for on the RT/10 could be addressed now – more cooling air for the brakes and less for the engine, for one. There were also changes in technology outside of Chrysler, such as infrared reflective headlamps, which were brighter than standard halogens but cost less and were easier to package than high-intensity discharge (HID) units (the latter were still rare at the time). Smaller airbags were now available, making it possible to have an airbag in the 14in (35.6cm) steering wheel and on the passenger side.

Safety standards were still moving, but so were computer modeling techniques. The GTS and later roadsters had 2in-thick blocks of high density foam to spread any side impact over a larger area of the safety bars; door parts were reinforced for safety, and to handle the weight of their full frames and glass windows. A clever addition was a theft alarm which monitored the ignition and anything that opened; the alarm flashed the headlights, honked the horn for 150 seconds, and disabled the fuel-injection. Any thief trying to use a slide hammer on the ignition switch would find a disabled car when they were done.

New woven-nylon airbags let air escape after deployment, while chemicals stayed inside – in prior airbags, the driver could be hurt by the explosives' residue (these had first been used in the Neon). One-way air vents in the car prevented airbag detonation from spiking air pressure, and made it easier to close the doors when all the windows were up. ACR buyers also got a standard five-point harness in addition to the usual production-car seatbelts, on the assumption that they would be taking their car to the track.

While the GTS had been thoroughly redesigned under the skin, the outward appearance was "RT/10 with a fixed roof." The aerodynamics told a more complete story: the roadster had a cD (coefficient of drag) of 0.495, which was fairly high for a modern car. The soft top brought it down to 0.46; with the fiberglass top, it was 0.45. These numbers were similar to the various K-car derivatives and, for that matter, Dodge's 1994 pickup trucks.

With the GTS, the coefficient of drag was just 0.35 – and it had more downforce. The more slippery shape brought a higher top speed (189mph, or 304km/h) and far less noise in the cabin; highway fuel economy improved a little, too.

Dodge reported that 1996 GTS with air-conditioning weighed 100lb (45kg) less than a 1994 RT/10 without it. The GTS weighed only 6lb more than the contemporary Porsche 911 Turbo, which was powered by a much smaller 3.6L six-cylinder engine (albeit one pushing out 400hp, or 298kW).

A new federal regulation had come into effect, requiring oxygen sensors both before and after the catalytic converter; Chrysler couldn't find a sensor that could stand the heat with the existing system, so Team Viper changed the exhaust to a conventional out-the-back routing. That improved the engine sound and lowered the back pressure, helping net power ratings.

The final 300 1995 RT/10s were stamped "Last 300 Sidepipes" on the passenger toe-box, according to Jon Brobst; the 1996 RT/10 had the same exhaust routing as the 1996 GTS.

IN PRODUCTION AND SHOWING OFF

The new GTS Coupe's paint scheme was a reflection of Peter Brock's Cobra Daytona; but even Peter Brock said the Viper stood on its own, despite the similarities. In Tom Gale's words, "There wasn't a surface on the car that was even close, or remotely like, a Cobra" – even though many thought there was a resemblance, outside of the paint and stripes.

To show off the car to journalists, Dodge brought a pack of writers over to famed European racing tracks; the press drove 18 Viper GTS Coupes between the racing sites. Peter Brock and other major racing personalities came along, talking with the media. The trip started in the United States, with Johnny Rutherford giving rides at the Indy track. In Europe, journalists drove prototype GTS coupes between and around the tracks; François Castaing reportedly urged them to go faster and harder. Jon Brobst said that the press people were afraid that two or three of the media people would crash the cars, particularly at Nürburgring; but while a couple of people ran out of gas, none of the media people crashed (ironically, a hired Formula One driver did).

This was the Viper that would expand the definition of the car's capabilities. Everyone knew it had a monster torque engine, but not everyone knew it could go around corners. Despite a good privateer effort at Le Mans, nobody knew it would soon be beating Ferraris and Porsches on their own turf. Dodge changed the minds of the motor media first, and then worked on the public.

The Viper GTS was chosen as the pace car for the Indy 500; this time, it was driven by Bob Lutz. The company supplied four Vipers, including a giveaway car, along with a large number of official trucks – Dodge "Indy Rams" with a matching paint-and-stripe job. Limited-edition versions of the pickup were available to the general public.

In what was to become a Viper tradition, the company gave roadster buyers first crack at the new coupes. 1996 production was estimated at 1700, and vouchers were sent to all current Viper owners. Those who already owned an RT/10 turned out to buy more than three-quarters of the 1996 GTS run. (Actual 1996 production was 1887 – 721 roadsters, 1166 coupes.) The first retail delivery of a Dodge Viper GTS was on June 8, 1996, to Jon Brobst of PartsRack.

There were new color schemes for this year: white with blue stripes and white wheels, red with yellow wheels, and black with silver stripes and silver wheels. The front and rear suspensions switched to the new GTS Coupe's aluminum parts, saving weight, and the frame was swapped out for the new GTS frame.

THE VIPER CLUB OF AMERICA

There were numerous Viper lovers even before they hit production. One, Jon Brobst, now owner of Viper-only store PartsRack, had been a British car enthusiast; he had been to Coventry to see Jaguars being built, and, after getting a Lotus Esprit Turbo, had been to Norwich to see those being built. When the Viper was shown in Detroit, he changed his vanity plate to VENOMUS, and sent in a deposit check and a letter; Chrysler wrote him back to say it couldn't take deposits, but would let him know when orders started.

True to its word, Chrysler sent Jon and the others a notice and list of local dealers with the car when the Viper was released. He called around, and found that the dealers who knew about the Viper were demanding double the sticker price – $110,000 for the $55,000 car. Jon said, "I wrote a crabby letter back to Chrysler, saying that I thought I was going to get my first American-built Chrysler sports car, but the dealers are too greedy. Bill Tracy, the head of Dodge Motorsports and Performance Marketing, faxed back, 'We're going to find you a dealer that will sell you a Viper at the sticker price.'"

That dealer was Latham Dodge of Twin Falls, Idaho, a small and isolated town quite a distance from Jon's Oregon home. Still, Jon was set to leave for Idaho when his local dealer called to say he'd like to sell the car at sticker price – the same car Jon had been trying to buy for months – to get it out of the inventory. Jon called Eric Lee, the salesman in Idaho, to tell him the story for its amusement value; but Eric asked Jon to take the Oregon offer, because Latham Dodge could sell that Viper for a $10,000 premium to someone else.

Jon ended up getting the car locally after all; but he sent more people to Eric Lee at Latham Dodge, in Twin Falls, Idaho, and at least three of them got Vipers from the little shop. Eric Lee eventually sold enough new and used Vipers that he started to call himself "Mr Viper."

Meanwhile, Jon had his new Viper. He recalled, "I almost crashed it coming home, it was just so scary fast. The next week, I enrolled in a performance driving school – and I had thought I was a pretty good driver."

Jon started using his Viper as a pace car at tracks in the northwest and California; the first week he owned the car, he called the number in the glove compartment (on a sticker labeled "Built with pride in Motor City by Team Viper") to ask about the best oil, tire pressure, and alignment settings. On the other end of the line was Herb Helbig, who said, "We built this car for guys like you. Tell me what you're doing. I want to know everything."

After the first Viper Owners Invitational, a national gathering hosted by Dodge in 1994, Viper marketing manager Ron Smith spent two weeks with Viper owner/enthusiast Maurice Liang to find the ideal place to hold the second Invitational. Liang suggested that Smith help create a national Viper club, and on Smith's request,

provided a detailed proposal with a national structure with affiliated local clubs.

Liang's proposal led to a May 1995 meeting of Ron Smith and 14 Viper enthusiast-owners, gathered together in Michigan; Liang recalled that he invited Chrysler president Bob Lutz as a courtesy, and "about fell out of my chair when his administrative assistant called me to RSVP that he would be attending our kick-off dinner!"

During their time in Michigan, they met Bob Lutz, Dodge chief Marty Levine, and other leaders, and toured the factory. The group elected Maurice Liang, a graduate of electrical and electronics engineering from the University of Michigan, to be the first national president, since he was already leading the charge and had held local club gatherings. Steve Ferguson, who had also held local gatherings, was elected national vice president; and, later, Jon Brobst was elected national secretary. Only two of the owners had past Dodge motorsports experience: Jon Brobst and professional tuner John Hennessey.

Ron Smith arranged to have Dodge's ad agency, JR Thompson, manage day-to-day club affairs, since it was already publishing *Viper Quarterly* magazine and managing the Viper Owners Invitationals. The 14 representatives became presidents for their respective regions.

Liang served as national president for two years, and was president of the Northern California Region for 20 years. He published *Snake Eyes*, a club magazine, for 20 years, and went on to write three books (*The Viper Buyer's Guide*, *SRT Viper – America's Supercar Returns*, and *Viper – 25 Years of Hisssstory*). Jon Brobst served as regional president for nine years, and was a national officer for three terms; he also became owner of PartsRack Inc, which catered exclusively to Viper owners.

Dodge supported the national club office, published *Viper Quarterly*, hosted the Viper Owners Invitationals for many years, and included a one year membership in the club with every new Viper. It was not a new or unique idea; BMW had been giving away memberships in its owners' club for some years, and had supported the club to the point of shipping American officers to Germany to drive new cars or photograph races. Still, it was a wild move for Chrysler.

A year after Daimler-Benz AG took over Chrysler Corporation, renaming the combined organization DaimlerChrysler, it balked at the expense of supporting the club; the cars started to include a surcharge ('marketing costs') to cover a first year's membership for the Viper Club of America, starting in 2000. Later, Dodge changed the system so new car buyers still got the free year's membership, but they had to send in a postcard to claim it, an arrangement that lasted until 2010.

Dodge advertised the Viper Club of America in its brochures for 1996 through 1999; in 2010, when it devoted a full brochure page to 'Viper Nation' – an

Creating the Viper Club of America: facing the camera, from left to right, are Maurice Liang (running the meeting), Dean Word, Kevin Tedder, Jim Roppo, John Hennessey, John Thompson, and Ron Smith. (Courtesy Maurice Liang)

Jon Brobst (left) and Ron Smith in 1996; Jon had just won the first-ever Viper Club autocross at Sebring. (Courtesy Maurice Liang)

undefined group which, it wrote, included over 25,000 owners and 100,000 other enthusiasts. It also promoted Viper Days in the brochure, and sponsored Viper Racing League events with professional drivers at reserved tracks. Dodge printed up club brochures and put them into the glove box, helping owners to get together and help each other with repairs, upgrades, maintenance, and racing and show opportunities. The Viper Club of America may have helped to keep sales high enough to sustain the car for more than ten years past its original sell-by date.

STREET-LEGAL: VIPER GT2 AND ACR

The Viper GTS was lauded on the covers of all sorts of magazines; though some pointed to its flaws, they also spoke highly of its strengths. But as it started to rack up racing successes, Team Viper responded with some special editions.

The first of these, the 1998 GT2 Championship Edition Viper, was a run of just 100 cars (enough to allow for SCCA club racing); it was street-legal, with the GTS-R paint scheme and an aerodynamic package including fascia drive plates, a front splitter, rear wing, and black sill-mounted ground effects. The GT2 had a name banner on the windshield and the sides of the hood; an American

flag and the words 'FIA GT2 Champion' were on a decal on the upper quarter panel. The package also included unique single-piece 18in wheels, with a Viper logo on the center caps, shod in Michelin MXX3 tires. Inside was a black interior with blue accents, a dash plaque, and the restraint system used by the Le Mans team.

The engine had a mild boost, from 450hp (336kW) to 460hp (343kW) at the same 5200rpm; torque rose from 490lb-ft (664Nm) to 500 (678Nm). Overall, the package would set a buyer back a hefty $85,200 including destination – but only 100 were made.

The next step, long overdue, may have been inspired by the success of the Dodge and Plymouth Neon in Sports Car Club of America (SCCA) racing. Neon ACR (American Club Racer) cars had won three consecutive national Class C Showroom Stock championships from 1995 to 1997. Neons won in Road Racing, Pro Rally, Pro Solo, Pro Solo II, and Super Solo from 1994 to 2004; the little car managed to win over 20 national titles, with 311 top-three finishes (in 216 national events) by the end of 1998.

The Neon's racing success was largely due to the inexpensive ACR package, which added adjustable shock absorbers (starting in 1997), performance wheels and

Your **key to the** **VIPER** **Experience**

GRAB LIFE BY THE HORNS

DODGE

Your key to the Viper Experience.

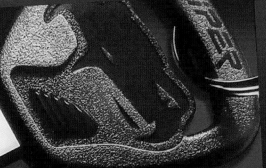

Your key to the Viper Experience.

Dodge Viper Different.

Maurice Liang in 2010. (Courtesy Maurice Liang)

Drive loudly and join a small club.

Obviously, owning and driving a Dodge Viper isn't for everyone. Those few who do, however, should know that there's an organization created especially for them.

Anyone who owns a Viper is automatically invited to join a unique group of automotive enthusiasts who have a great deal to be enthusiastic about. It's more than just owning the most soul-stirring set of wheels on the planet. It's about all you can do with your Viper and fellow Viper owners.

Maybe you're interested in joining a local chapter of the Viper Clubs of America. Or participating in special club racing activities and tours. Or attending Viper Owners Invitationals in places like Las Vegas and Orlando. Or visiting the Viper assembly plant when you specify factory delivery of your new Viper (ask your dealer for details).

There's even an information-packed magazine especially for Viper owners and fans. Subscription and membership information can be obtained by calling 1-800-998-1110. And if you're interested in special Viper

apparel, including the jacket shown here, just call 1-888-267-2187 for a catalog.

So you can enjoy your ownership to the fullest, we suggest you consider attending a performance driving school such as the Dodge-Skip Barber Driving School and the Skip Barber Racing School who have chosen Dodge as the exclusive supplier of vehicles and engines for all their teaching and racing operations. For information, e-mail speed@skipbarber.com, call 1-800-221-1131, or visit the Web site at www.skipbarber.com.

DODGE
Skip Barber

The Ownership Experience

Being a Viper owner involves much more than simply purchasing or even driving a Viper. Because taking delivery on a Viper GTS Coupe or RT-10 Roadster is only the beginning.

Viper owners are a special breed. Once you've joined the Viper ownership body, you become part of a commonwealth of Viper owners, with members all over the world. Many belong to local Viper Clubs of America chapters, which take part in various Viper-related activities. It's a great way to share in the excitement and camaraderie of Viper ownership.

For example, there's a Viper Invitational, where Viper owners are invited to participate with Dodge on an annual basis, sharing in the latest information from Team Viper. Activities include high-energy banquets with special guest speakers, technical sessions, seminars, entertainment and on-track driving programs. Dodge also publishes a special magazine for its owners called *Viper Quarterly*. It's filled with the latest information on Viper, gathered from knowledgeable sources within Dodge, Team Viper and aftermarket suppliers. For more information about Dodge Viper, or to be put on the Viper mailing list, contact 1-800-4-A-DODGE.

Viper Club meeting, San Diego, California.

The Viper Invitational, 1996.

The Viper Quarterly

28

29

Opposite left, above, and next page: Dodge advertised the VCA in Viper brochures. (Courtesy Maurice Liang)

tires, beefier sway bars, front brake coolers using the foglight holes, an unlimited-speed engine computer, a bigger radiator, and a specially geared transmission.

Dodge finally created a second ACR package, the 1999 Dodge Viper ACR, for the GTS. Dodge chief Jim Julow said it had learned from the GT2 that "there is a previously untapped demand for limited-production, motorsports derivatives of the Viper." It was a serious package, not a stripe kit: the cars had no stereo or air-conditioning, and had lighter wheels and shock absorbers, so they could drop 60lb (27kg) of weight. The Neon ACR's trick of replacing fog lights with brake cooling ducts was adopted to the Viper. Customers could buy it in any GTS color.

The Viper ACR used GTS-R springs (supplied by Meritor, née Rockwell) and gas-charged Koni racing shock absorbers, adjustable for bump and rebound. The front

stabilizer bar had a 1.06in (27mm) diameter, while the rear bar had a 0.86in (22mm) diameter. The single-piece, 18in BBS wheels had the usual front and rear widths, and were shod with Michelin Pilot Sport radials – P275/35ZR18 in front, and P335/30ZR18 in back. The engine had a K&N air filter and smoother air-cleaner hoses (for lower air resistance). Inside, buyers had the GTS-R's five-point restraint system. The ground clearance was 5.0 inches (127mm); curb weight was listed as 3356lb (1525kg), though if buyers opted to put the air-conditioning and audio back in, it ended up at 3403lb (1547kg). Weight distribution was 48/52.

Sales of 400 1999 Viper ACRs beat Dodge's expectations, and the package returned for 2000-2002 with some improvements, including a performance oil pan, new nameplates, and Dynamic Suspensions adjustable monotube shock absorbers. The Dodge Viper ACR Plus had Mopar aftermarket parts installed to produce over 500hp and 530lb-ft of torque.

CHANGES

Roy Sjoberg left his role at Chrysler in January 1997 and started working as a consulting engineer; one of his tasks was to homologate the new Maserati for the United States. In 2004, he became president of vehicle operations for Heart International, working on a hybrid SUV and military vehicle for the US Army. He raced in SCCA/IMSA as a hobby, and traveled with his wife, Peg, visiting Concours d'Elegance in various places. Today, he owns Team R-Squared S LLP, which does auto consulting and makes some aftermarket parts.

The 1997 Viper RT/10 had the rest of the GTS coupe's improvements, with interior and powertrain upgrades to match the GTS, including outside door handles and power windows. Color schemes were Viper GTS Blue with white stripes and Viper Red; buyers could get a gold wheel package. Production of the new roadsters started in January 1997; Dodge made just 117 of them for this year, along with 1671 coupes.

1998 was a bad year for Chrysler enthusiasts, with Daimler-Benz AG taking the company over mid-year, but it was a good year for Vipers. They gained lighter exhaust manifolds that heated up faster, so the catalyst hit operating temperature more quickly; and tubular stainless steel exhaust manifolds, always in the plan, replaced the cast iron ones, saving 24lb (11kg) on both RT/10 and GTS.

A new reduced-overlap camshaft allowed for increased spark advance at idle, making it smoother. Other changes included a silver paint option (with or without blue stripes), passenger airbag on/off switch, next-generation airbags which deployed with less force, and more secure locks and keyless entry systems. The computer was put in control of the radiator fan (a newer, quieter model) and alternator to reduce parasitic losses, and new windshield washer nozzles resisted freeze-up for the hard-core Viper owner.

Dodge made 379 RT/10s and 837 GTS coupes, for a total of 1216 cars in the 1998 model year; buyers could choose between red and silver. Black, green, and yellow were no longer available.

The '99s gained 18in aluminum wheels with Viper-logo center caps and Michelin Pilot Sport tires. On March 1, 1999, Dodge added frame reinforcements to prevent cracking of the differential support brackets and steering gear crossmember under aggressive driving. As reinforced, the roadster frame had a torsional rating of 6400lb-ft (8677Nm) per degree – an improvement over the already strong 5000lb-ft of the original 1992 roadsters.

Other changes for 1999 included moving to 18in wheels, with Viper-logo center caps and Michelin Pilot Sport tires. Production was 549 RT/10s, 484 GTS, and 215 ACRs, a total of 1248. Colors were red, black, and steel silver.

For 2000, Steel Gray was added to the color list, and child seat tethers, now mandatory, were added.

(continued on page 50)

Yellow Vipers debuted in 1994. (Courtesy Marc Rozman)

Hypereutectic pistons, which were lighter and didn't expand as much with heat, made the engine a little more responsive. Buyers could opt for a Mopar aftermarket CD changer ($345), red Viper storage bag ($60), or "car bra" ($148). Dodge made 840 roadsters, 731 coupes, and 218 ACRs for a total of 1789 2000 Vipers. It also showed off a red-with-gray-stripes Competition Coupe concept, which hinted at the appearance of the 2003 Viper SRT-10.

Sophisticated four-wheel antilock brakes, with electronic brake-force distribution, were standard in the 2001 Vipers; by now, antilock brakes were pretty much required among supercars, and they helped bring down the Viper's braking distance to that of the rest of the pack.

Color choices were yellow, red, and sapphire blue (a relatively dark shade, compared with the old GTS Blue), with optional black center stripes on the yellow GTS. By this time, Dodge had sold over 10,000 Vipers: a higher number than most onlookers expected from the specialty sports car. 2001 model-year production was 874 roadsters, 650 coupes, and 227 ACRs, a total of 1751.

To summarize the coupe colors: the 1996 Viper GTS was available in blue with white stripes. For 1997, buyers could get a yellow wheel package and blue or red paint. For 1998, Dodge added red with silver stripes, and silver with optional blue stripes. Black (with or without silver stripe) joined the list for 1999, along with a Cognac Connolly leather option group; and steel gray showed up in 2000. The 2001 buyers saw a new Viper Race Yellow option (with or without black center stripes), and a new blue option (a neat touch for the 2001 buyers was having the Viper logo molded into the key heads). Finally, the 2002 had a choice of graphite metallic paint with optional silver stripes; yellow with optional black stripes, or red with optional silver stripes.

THE LAST OF THE FIRST GENERATIONS

When Dodge issued its 2002 press releases, it wrote: "The 2002 Dodge Viper RT/10 Roadster and GTS Coupe – representing the first and second chapters in the legendary story of the Viper – will mark the final model year for one of the most outrageous cars ever produced by a major automotive manufacturer. To commemorate the turning of the page, Dodge will offer 2002 Vipers in a rich new Graphite metallic paint, with silver stripes available on GTS models."

The last 2002 Viper press release touted its 450hp (335kW) and 490lb-ft (664 Nm), unchanged from the 1996 launch. Perhaps unwisely, it also noted, "an all-new version of the supercar will debut for 2003." With that tease out in the open, Dodge reportedly had a hard time selling the 2002 Vipers.

The final 360 Viper coupes were part of a "GTS Final Edition," painted in red with white stripes and carrying special badges (all were coupes; 34 were ACRs). Why did it make 360 Final Editions? Perhaps it was in homage to the V8 engine that was the original basis for the Viper's V10; more likely, it was an estimate of what the plant could build, given plant capacity and parts contracts. One source claimed the Final Edition was an attempt to sell otherwise unwanted Vipers to collectors, as most buyers were awaiting the '03s. For similar reasons, a number of Viper RT/10 roadsters were sent out to private vendors for conversion to right-hand drive and sale in Australia, New Zealand, and Japan.

Dodge made 545 roadsters, 759 coupes, and 159 ACRs in the final year of the first generation; they were available in red, yellow, and graphite metallic. 1463 cars was a good sendoff for the final year of the first Chrysler V10 production car ever.

4

First-generation Viper engines and transmissions

Developing an engine usually takes several years. Engineers test different combustion chambers, check out competing engines' technologies and designs, set up the basic architecture, and run thousands of hours of tests, starting with single-cylinders and slowly moving up.

The Viper engine was specified when the prototype program was authorized in 1989; the car was to be unveiled in January 1992. The engine team, headed by Jim Royer, included design engineer Charlie Brown, development engineer Dick Winkles, and designers Pete Kinsler and Bob Zeimis; the retired head of engine design, Willem Weertman, came in as a consultant. Racing engine developer Heini Mader (founder of HMP) worked on reducing friction, and Bill Hancock of race-engine builder Arrow Engineering provided "primary engine assistance," according to Team Viper. Chrysler would work with Arrow (later operating as Prefix) throughout the Viper program, from generation to generation.

The timing was almost insane by normal standards, but they had a starting point: the Chrysler 360 cubic inch V8 engine. It's worth taking a few minutes to explore the that venerable powerplant.

Chrysler Corporation was engineering-driven from the creation of the 1904 Maxwell; but engineering became its defining characteristic once three superb engineers (Fred Zeder, Owen Skelton, and Carl Breer) took power, putting research and development at the forefront. The scientific method became the company's driving force, and such niceties as styling and "we've always done it that way" were, for a time, discarded. The original 1924 Chrysler car was a breakthrough, and the company went from success to success. Its wartime accomplishments were almost unbelievable, from re-engineering Bofors guns and producing them at rates and costs far, far better than anyone's expectations, to rescuing the atomic bomb project.

Experience from creating a powerful aviation engine (rendered obsolete before its first test flight by jets) led to Chrysler's first V8 engine, which had hemispherical chambers with large ports on opposing sides. The first of these 'double rockers,' later known as 'Hemis,' were developed under James Zeder, Ray White, Mel Carpentier, William Drinkard, and Ev Moeller. They were influenced by the Riley four-cylinder engine (used by Healey), which had greater power than the Ford V8; but they went above and beyond. The new engines were efficient, long-lived, and tolerant of low-quality fuel; but they were also expensive, heavy, wide, and slow to produce.

The engine started out as a Chrysler-brand exclusive in 1951, moving to DeSoto and Dodge in 1952. V8 engines were soon required in the mainstream cars, so the engineers tried replacing the dual-rocker Hemi heads with single-rocker polyspherical heads on some engines. It wasn't enough, so they gave up and went to the wedge-type design used by Ford and Chevrolet. The efficiency loss was not as large as they'd thought, and these new 'A' engines – still using blocks based on the 1951 Chrysler 'Fire Power' double-rocker V8 – became the company's mainstay.

The engineers then used new casting technologies to cut weight from the design, and to increase durability and power. The result was the 'Lightweight A,' or LA, engines; these were, by far, the most popular Chrysler V8s into the 1990s. People remember Chrysler's 383 'B' engine, 440 'RB' engine, and 426 Hemi fondly; but, in the 1960s and 1970s, they were far more likely to actually own an LA engine.

The first of the LA engines was the 273 (273ci, or 4.5L), which was quickly expanded to 318ci (5.2L). Next up was a performance version, the 340 (5.6L); and then a longer-stroke version, with a bore between that of the 318 and 340,

meant mainly for trucks and to replace the big 383 (6.3L) in large cars. This motor, displacing 360ci (5.9L), would soon replace the 340 as the company's small performance V8, then become the company's only performance V8. During the 1980s, it became a truck-only engine.

The 360 was improved almost continuously over the years; in the 1989 Dodge trucks, the carburettor was replaced by a pair of throttle-body fuel injectors, yielding the 'truck engine' Bob Lutz didn't think suitable for his Cobra (as produced in 1989, it really wasn't). Within a few years, sequential multiple-port fuel-injection replaced the throttle-body injectors, dramatically increasing power and efficiency. Chrysler made the 360 through December 2002, a remarkable run for a derivative of Chrysler's very first, 1951-vintage V8 engine; but it's unlikely many internal parts could be swapped between a 1951 'Fire Power' and a 2002 '5.9 Magnum.'

As we recalled in Chapter 1, Dodge was already working on a V10 version of the 360 V8 for its trucks, which were largely selling on the strength of their Cummins ISB diesel enigines. The ISB was a strong, durable, efficient motor, but it was expensive; a big gasoline engine would be cheaper, but still have the high low-end torque buyers got from the Cummins, and some of the durability as well. In the Viper, the truck V10 would be far too heavy, with far too much torque and too little horsepower.

Chrysler's 1951 V8 Hemi, 'Fire Power' engine. (Author)

Cross-ram wedge V8 engine in a 1960 Chrysler 300F: Beautiful and effective, but impractical for daily drivers and many races. (Author)

Reportedly, the Viper and truck V10s did not share a single part; but both had the same starting points and the same irregular firing intervals of 90° and 54°.

LAMBORGHINI STEPS IN

The Viper team's deadline was a full 18 months earlier than that of the truck group, with its less-challenging iron-block V10. François Castaing thought they could make their deadlines with help from one of Lee Iacocca's acquisitions – Lamborghini. Specifically, Castaing thought Mauro Forghieri, who had been lured to the exotic automaker from Ferrari, could do the trick.

Dick Winkles had been to Lamborghini's headquarters, as part of Chrysler's program to share skills with that company; various engineers were sent to Italy, staying there from a few months to a year. Dick had hoped to use Lamborghini's V10 engine control system on the Chrysler truck motor, but he discovered that the cost was far too high to be practical.

Team Viper sent over its truck engine drawings, and asked Lamborghini to make whatever changes were needed for an aluminum block. According to Roy Sjoberg, Lamborghini was to use its prototyping equipment to deliver five running engines; in the end, it only made two or three V10 engines in Italy, to be dressed and tested back in Michigan.

Willem Weertman confirmed that Lamborghini did the initial conversion to aluminum, and, in the words of Weertman's book *Chrysler Engines*, the Italian automaker provided "a small number of machined parts and a number of additional castings. After this initial brief participation by Lamborghini, the activity and entire responsibility of the Viper engine program was assumed by the Viper engine group."

Chris Theodore said that Mauro Forghieri was the primary designer in the Lamborghini effort, but he specified a Formula One-style cooling system with short water jackets, which, for a car meant to be run on the street, "was a disaster."

Chrysler's needs were very different from those of Ferrari or Lamborghini: it had a larger production runs, definite cost constraints, more durability testing, and expectations of 100,000 essentially trouble-free miles (around 160,000km). The Viper engine had to run well in very cold and very hot weather; it needed to run 300 hours at wide-open throttle on the dyno, and to simply start-up and run, with no problems.

None of the Lamborghini-specified parts made it to production; Chrysler found less exotic helpers in its supplier base. Still, everyone liked the way the engine looked, and it kept as much of Lamborghini's styling as it could, along with Lamborghini's external coolant manifold. That was, essentially, a cast passage outside each cylinder bank, with pipes for each cylinder; after cooling the cylinders, coolant went to the heads and then returned to the radiator.

TEAM VIPER TAKES OVER

Once Lamborghini had weighed in, the engine was developed in Michigan, entirely on computer, using the truck V8 as a starting point.

Chrysler had pioneered cross-ram air intakes in the 1960s; beautiful and impractical, they made a definite impression. Their long tubes gracefully crossed from the air cleaners on one side of the engine bay to the cylinder bank on the opposite side, crossing in the middle; the goal was to use a supercharging effect to boost power at certain engine speeds.

The Viper was set up along the same lines, to a lesser degree. Its intake manifold was created from two cast bases, two cast air plenums, and ten formed tubes, brazed together into a single unit. The base castings included a fuel delivery run, feeding the five injectors on each side; at the other end were twin 60mm throttle bodies, bolted on and connected to a balance tube. It was an attractive configuration if not quite as grand or ostentatious as the 'cross-ram Wedge.' It was impressively compact, helping the Viper engine to have a lower height than any Chrysler V8, ever – under 26in (66cm).

The basic engine structure carried over from the old 360 V8, complete with the 90° angle between the cylinder banks. The bore and stroke were 4.00x3.88in (101.6x98.6mm), yielding a displacement of 488cid (7994 cc); the bore was between the old 318 and 360, while the stroke was effectively longer because the forged aluminum pistons were only 1.38in (35mm) tall.

Bore spacing was 4.55in (11.56cm); the deck height was 9.48in (24.08cm), somewhat lower than the V8; and the block was machined to exactly 28in (71.1cm) in length. It was a deep skirt (3.50in, or 8.89cm) design, to handle high power without flexing.

Using an aluminum block and heads saved around a 100lb (45kg) over the truck engine; the weight came in at 711-716lb, or 322-324kg (depending on the source) in the 1992 Viper R/T 10. By the time the 1996 GTS was out, they were able to drop another 80lb (36kg).

Chrysler used time-tested cast iron liners, with twin O-rings at the bottom to seal the crankcase cavity and coolant jacket. The aluminum heads were sand-cast, with iron-alloy inserts for valve seats and press-fitted valve stem guides; the valve seat inserts were shrink-fitted.

Some wanted a four-valve-per-cylinder engine, or at least one without pushrods; but there was little time or money for such niceties. Chrysler's first four-valve-per-cylinder engine ended up being the four-cylinder 'Turbo III,' used in the Spirit R/T and Daytona R/T – high performers for the day, with over 10hp per cc from 2.2L. One thing the two engines would share was distributorless ignition.

The team encountered hot spots in the heads, and with time at a premium, they compensated by dropping the compression from 10:1 to 9.1:1; that also allowed owners to use midgrade (89 US octane), rather than

Viper intake tubes crossing over the block. (Courtesy Angela Puckett)

Viper crate engine sold by Chrysler's aftermarket group. (Courtesy Mopar)

premium (91 US octane), fuel. By the time the 1996 GTS came out, they had resolved the cooling issues, and were able to bring up the compression.

The intake valves, one per cylinder, were a generous 1.92in (4.88cm) in diameter, with 1.58in (4.01cm) exhaust valves, at an 18° angle from the cylinder centerlines – as they had been in the very first 273cid (4.5L) LA engines. Another gift from the older engines was a set of forged steel connecting rods, as used in the existing V8, albeit shot-peened and tested before use. Valve lash was automatically adjusted by hydraulic roller tappets, and the valve covers were magnesium.

The new engine had a forged crankshaft, with 3in (76mm) diameter main journals and 2⅛in (54mm) diameter crank pins; the crank pins shared dimensions with Chrysler

small-block V8s going back to 1956. Weertman said that the original design had six main bearing caps, created as a single aluminum casting, and connected by panels that acted as a windage tray. When that did not work out, they switched to separate iron bearing caps and a separate sheet metal windage tray connected by brackets to the caps.

Highland Park headquarters' dynamometers (dynos) were nearly all designed for standard-performance engines; only one cell, the famed Cell 13, run by Dick Winkles and Bob Zimas and used for racing motors, could deal with high-performance engines.

Most Chrysler suppliers were oriented towards mass production, but they could use the Viper as a testbed for new technologies – which is one reason why it had a bottom-fed fuel-injection system, the first the company

Viper GTS-R engine, bolted into a racing car. (Author)

had used. That system ran cooler than a top-feed setup, allowed the fuel rail to be cast as part of the intake manifold, and were less likely to trap fuel vapor than a standard setup. By the 1993 model-year, bottom-feed injection was on a completely different engine, the new 3.5L premium V6.

Packaging a V10 in a small sports car was always going to be a challenge, and there were many ways to make it work. The belt-driven accessories, for example, were attached to the timing chain cover; and the radiator had dimpled coolant tubes to increase heat transfer, so it could be smaller and lighter.

Other clever ideas included the design of the cold air intake and oil pan. Starting with the 1996 GTS, the cold air intake had a duct on the edge of the hood; water was separated by baffles and spring-loaded drains which were opened by the weight of the water. The oil pan was cast so the intake was at the bottom of the pan, with a baffle guiding oil towards the intake, so it could have a shallow oil pan which would not run dry under hard cornering. An auxiliary oil cooler was placed in front of the radiator, and the oil pump was built into the timing chain cover and driven by the crankshaft.

As noted before, Chrysler did not have an electronics system for a V10 when the Viper went into production; insane as it sounds, it combined a V6 engine unit with a four-cylinder unit to bridge the two-year gap between the Viper and the availability of the truck V10 computer.

The firing order (1-10-9-4-3-6-5-8-7-2) and timing were the same as in the truck engine; the crankpins were separated by 72°, which brought unequal firing intervals

of 90° and 54°. Willem Weertman said they were concerned about the sound and feel, but it worked out well and the very last Viper engine had the same intervals.

Another marvel of size was the new metal-monolithic catalytic converters, which were about 40% smaller than standard units. That brings us to one of the biggest challenges – the side exhausts. There was little space for them, and catalytic converters generate a huge amount of heat (over 1000°F or 538°C).

The exhaust headers were tuned to boost power at 2000-4000rpm; they were made from two fabricated sections of thin-walled, vacuum-cast steel alloy manifold, an upper section (with five branches, and identical for both sides of the car) and a lower section including oxygen sensors. The two sections were bolted together and connected to a 2.5in (6.35cm)-diameter exhaust pipe.

They couldn't get the noise down below the required 80dB while tuning the sound, and the heat made it impossible to have the exposed headers of the concepts and early prototypes. Twin 3mm Nomex layers shielded the outer sill; the floorpan was lined as well, to avoid melting the carpet.

By mid-1990, the Viper V10 was pushing out just 380hp (283kW) with 510lb-ft (691Nm) of torque. That would have been good for a truck, but there was too little horsepower for a car, and too much torque for the transmission, which was rated at 460lb-ft (624Nm). The LA family had been designed for heavy cars and for trucks, after all.

Output on the 1992-93 cars ended up at 400hp (298kW) at 4600rpm and 450lb-ft (610Nm) of torque at

3600rpm, still more torque-biased than the team had wanted; but time only permitted so much tuning. By comparison, the 1993 Corvette ZR-1 had a little more horsepower (405hp, or 302kW) but drivers had to rev to 5800rpm to get it; they had 385lb-ft (522Nm) of torque, but again, drivers had to rev the engine further to get to the 4800rpm peak. The two cars shared the same basic manual transmission; the Corvette cost over $10,000 more, and was around 100lb (around 45kg) heavier. For that matter, the 1965 Shelby Cobra 427SC used a non-emissions cast iron engines, optimistically rated at 425hp (317kW) and a hefty 480lb-ft (651Nm) of torque – but those were gross figures, before engine accessories were added in. A typical engine dropped 40-50hp when going from gross to net, and the muscle car era engine ratings were often, shall we say, 'looser' than modern numbers; small changes in tuning could also drop the peak numbers quite a bit.

In any case, Viper drivers had 400lb-ft (532Nm) on tap at just 1200rpm; that kind of torque permitted taller top gearing, helping US highway mileage ratings to reach 21mpg (11L/100km).

Roy Sjoberg recalled, "We loved that engine. We called it the BFM, Big Freakin' Motor."

BUILDING ENGINES

Parts of the Viper V10 had to be made outside of the company, because of its low volume and higher precision. Jim Royer chose high-speed CNC machining to make the engines and some chassis components, which were outsourced to "a little company out in Howell, Michigan."

The first engine was assembled on March 2, 1992, at the Mound Road engine plant – birthplace and still home of the LA series V8s. Issues with head gasket failure in these early motors could be resolved by replacing the paper/fiber gaskets with MLS versions, and using new head bolts (the MLS gasket required more torque on the bolts).

The 1994-95 engines had the same horsepower ratings, but the 1994 press release and 1995 dealer information sheet listed torque as being 480lb-ft (651Nm) at 3600rpm, presumably in error? The 1995 press release showed torque at 465lb-ft (626Nm), the only change being replacement of the brazed intake manifold with

V10 in context. (Courtesy Angela Puckett)

a single-piece casting (at the time of writing, Wikipedia showed 462lb-ft). The 1995 Viper brochure claimed a 0-60mph time of 4.4 seconds and a 0-100-0 time of 17.2 seconds, along with a 1.0 lateral g-force in a 300-foot circle and top speed of 165mph.

Can we make sense of this? Willem Weertman, in his comprehensive and well-researched *Chrysler Engines* book, confirmed the 400hp/450lb-ft figures reported earlier. He reported the 1995 intake change, saying the output of the engine was not affected by it; and, like the 1996 press releases, he listed output of the modified, 1996 model-year version at 415hp and 488lb-ft , using premium fuel. (There was one slight difference, in the metric figures: the press release showed 309kW and 661Nm, while Weertman reported it as 310kW and 662Nm.)

The exhaust had been reworked to a conventional rear exit, dropping the back pressure, to comply with a federal mandate to add a post-catalyst oxygen sensor. There was no sensor on the market that could deal with the heat of the side pipes and still resist water when needed. Running the pipes into the muffler and out the back of the car solved the problem, and made a more pleasant engine note; a new insulated aluminum panel protected the trunk floor and the gas tank from exhaust heat. There was a single muffler; duals were ruled out due to lack of space.

The door sills were not quite as hot because the exhaust flowed through more quickly; and the change allowed for a lower-restriction muffler while still meeting federal noise rules.

THE TRUCK V10

What of the Dodge truck V10? The Dodge Ram's powerplant ended up with the broadest usable torque curve (from 1000 to 4000rpm) of any large gasoline engine in pickups, and gave the Ram 2500 faster acceleration than any other truck in its class – regardless of transmission, unloaded or loaded. It wasn't a sports car, but it could move a heavy load quite well.

The truck engine kept the V8's bore to reduce tooling costs and development time, but, like the Viper, it had direct ignition and a crankshaft-mounted oil pump. It also had returnless fuel-injection (which regulated fuel flow within the gas tank, so excess fuel wasn't sent all the way up to the engine bay and then sent back all the way to the gas tank.) which was unusual at the time, and a single two-barrel side-draft throttle body (as opposed to the Viper's twin throttle bodies).

The intake manifold was designed to boost torque from 1700 to 3300rpm, using 25in (635mm) primary runners; peak torque hit much earlier than on the Viper, at 1200rpm. With its larger bore and lower stroke, the truck ended up with the same 8.0L (488cid) displacement as the first Viper engines. Compression was lower (8.6:1) and horsepower was far lower, with ratings of 300hp (224kW) and 450lb-ft (610Nm) of torque. The 1996 Rams gained sequential multiple-port fuel-injection for better

drivability, economy, and emissions, but the power ratings did not change.

The truck V10 was used in the Dodge Ram 2500 and 3500 for nearly ten years. When it was dropped, the most powerful Ram gasoline engine was the 5.7L 'Hemi' V8, which was cheaper to make, lighter, and easier on fuel; it had just 375lb-ft (508Nm) on tap, but generated more horsepower (345hp, or 257kW). Its real replacement was the 2013 6.4L 'truck Hemi,' rated at 410hp (306kW) and 429lb-ft (582Nm).

A SEMI-SECOND GENERATION FOR THE GTS COUPE

By the time the 1996 Viper GTS Coupe was unveiled, Team Viper had worked out ways to improve the cooling, so they could boost the compression from 9.1:1 to 9.6:1; the new car also had a new cam, moving from an intake duration of 292.5° and an exhaust duration of 288.5° to an intake duration of 290° and a exhaust duration of 305°. That allowed increasing spark advance at idle without increased emissions.

Willem Weertman pointed out there were many changes to the V10 engine, still relatively new. The thick, replaceable bore liners were replaced with thin, non-replaceable bore liners, shrink-fitted into the block; bearing caps attached by four bolts were replaced with cross-bolted caps; and both vertical and horizontal bolts clamped the caps to the block, increasing rigidity. The new cross-bolted caps were both stronger and 2lb (0.91kg) lighter, per cap. The block itself was changed, with thinner walls.

A more precise technique for casting the heads reduced weight, and allowed thinner water jackets, speeding heat transfer; they were also able to move cooling passages closer to the hottest areas. As a side bonus, having less antifreeze helped the cars warm up more quickly. All these changes slashed 80lb (36kg) from the engine's weight, while other changes, including higher valve lifts, helped to boost output to 450hp (336kW) and 490lb-ft (664Nm) of torque.

Fabricated steel exhaust manifolds were finally ready for the 1998 Vipers, cutting weight by 24lb (11kg); the manifolds were lighter and heated up more quickly, 'lighting off' the catalytic converters earlier.

Hypereutectic pistons replaced the forged ones for 2000, cutting weight and heat expansion for better responsiveness.

TRANSMISSION

The transmission had to be strong, sturdy, and reasonably priced. Chrysler relied on Getrag for its other performance engines, but the V10 was in a different league from the turbo-fours. Still, transmission engineer Herb Helbig thought Getrag could have developed a transmission capable of dealing with the enormous torque; the American Getrag group had some ideas, but its German headquarters people refused to make any accommodations for high-speed clutch drops and speed shifting (changing gears without lifting the accelerator). To fix just one problem with the tail housing, Getrag reportedly wanted to both increase the price and charge millions for development. It simply wasn't in Team Viper's budget.

Longtime Jeep supplier BorgWarner, which had provided the Wagoneer's first transmissions, was in the midst of creating a new six-speed manual transmission for the Chevrolet Corvette.

Roy Sjoberg talked to some people at BorgWarner, who thought GM would not allow them to share it; so then he spoke with people at GM. It turned out that the massive automaker welcomed the idea of sharing the transmission, since it would lower its own costs; the Corvette team also knew that, in time, it would have more powerful engines and would need the same torque upgrades. BorgWarner devoted a team to keeping the transmission up to date with the Dodge and Chevy power boosts over the years, and both GM and Chrysler reaped the benefits.

The BorgWarner T-56 was a close-ratio design, with a computer-controlled 'skip-shift' to guide the shifter from first gear into fourth at low throttle; the abundant torque made it practical, and gas mileage made it advisable. The fourth gear was a direct, 1:1 ratio; fifth jumped up to 0.74:1, and sixth was a steep 0.5:1.

The transmission was a constant mesh design; all gears were always meshed with each other, preventing gear clash. The gear teeth had a special microfinish to make shifts easier and quieter. The Viper version used stainless steel synchronizers, while GM and Ford versions used brass.

When the car was in gear and under power, just the selected gear transferred power, while the others freewheeled – until engaged by a synchronizer sleeve. In neutral, with the engine running, all the gears turned, but none of the synchronizers were engaged, so no power reached the main shaft. The reverse block, once it arrived, was controlled by the computer.

Gear	T-56	TR-6060
First	2.66	2.26
Second	1.78	1.58
Third	1.30	1.19
Fourth	1.00	1.00
Fifth	0.741	0.77
Sixth	0.50	0.63

Power was pushed through a hydraulic 12-inch clutch and aluminum driveshaft to a limited slip Dana 44 differential, geared to a 3.07:1 ratio. The lubricant was GM's Dexron 3 automatic transmission fluid, but the factory eventually switched to Castrol Syntorq, a heavier, synthetic-based fluid. (Some owners reported problems after using alternate fluids, such as Mobil 1 ATF.)

The Dodge Viper was the first car to use the T-56, by less than a year; GM used it in the 1993 Camaro, Firebird, and Trans Am, and later in Corvettes. It was also used by two Aston Martins, the Ram SRT-10, Ford Mustang Cobra, and Cadillac CTS-V, among others.

The 1996-97 cars, could have some transmission rattling while in neutral; it didn't seem to affect performance or longevity. Some owners had it addressed under warranty; the factory resolved the issue in the '98s. Starting in 1998, the transmission was built by Tremec, though the design was unchanged – at least, until the 2003 Vipers came out.

1995 Viper GTS-R engine on display. (Author)

5

Fresh start: the 2003 Dodge Viper SRT-10

In 2002, Chrysler had stopped making its old LA V8s, and shut down the historic Mound Road plant; Viper engine production moved into the Conner Avenue plant. It was a good time for a redesign, using all the team had learned from racing the hottest European cars on the track.

One could ask why DaimlerChrysler would pay for a new sports car, when its cost cuts at Chrysler were reaching comical extremes. Dodge motorsports chief Jim Julow answered that question, noting that Viper owners extended their passion for the Viper to all things Dodge. Before the Viper, they were unlikely to own "Mopars," as Chrysler Corporation cars were sometimes known; then, after buying a Viper, "they'll have four or five vehicles in their fleet … which are a Chrysler Group product: mostly Dodges."

In short, the Viper created sales to demographic groups that Chrysler couldn't reach otherwise. That, and a healthy bottom line, probably sold the continued investment in the 2003 Viper to DaimlerChrysler. It may also be why Chrysler supported Viper clubs. The National Chrysler Products Club and Plymouth Owners' club had permission to use company trademarks in their name; the Viper Club of America was invited to tour the plant. When the 2003 Viper was launched, existing owners came first; the first year of production was sold to current Viper owners within 30 days.

There was not just a large, international Viper club, but also local clubs, arranging track days to race each other; as Julow said, this was a group worth courting.

MID-ENGINE ALTERNATIVE

In 1996, when a next-generation Viper began to look like a reality, François Castaing wanted to explore a mid-engine design to lower the center of gravity, put more weight onto the rear wheels, and boost Chrysler's reputation for innovation. Drawbacks included higher cost and development time; possible issues for less-experienced drivers, and changes to the appearance.

Since Roy Sjoberg was busy on the racing circuit, he asked Jim Sayen to provide a full detailed engineering cost analysis. The main question was: how many parts could be carried over unchanged, or with modifications, and how many new parts would be needed? To do the job properly,

Sayen and a few others created two mockups with the engine behind the driver (who would have heated seats all year round); they worked offsite, in a locked room, to avoid any rumors.

At this point, François Castaing was the executive vice president of engineering, Roy Sjoberg was the engineer in charge of the Viper project, and Chris Theodore was between them; the final decision would be up to Bob Lutz. Told they were going to present it to Lutz, Sayen and the team made the car look more like a prototype than an engineering mockup; the front fenders looked like the 1996 versions, with a similar gap between fender and door. Huge intakes sat just behind the doors, ready to feed the massive V10. The engine was under the slope of the rear window and the tilt of the driver's seat; some space was behind it, for the catalytic converters and exhaust.

In retrospect, Sayen said they might have made a mistake in making the car look too realistic; when people saw it, they thought it was a prototype. The purpose, again, was to find out what parts would be needed, and what problems might come up. As an example, keeping the transmission would require power to be routed via a driveshaft and transfer case, which would take space from the passenger side, so that a reasonably tall passenger (like Bob Lutz) would hit their head against the roof.

The team made the cars look all too realistic – and too good; though Design had not been called in, they looked ready for production, and some people found it hard to believe they hadn't been created for that purpose. In any case, Bob Lutz ended up rejecting the mid-engined idea – most likely due to the higher cost.

500+500+500

The headline news for the 2003 Viper, despite many other changes, was its revised engine: the V10 was now an alliterative 505 cubic inches, 500 horsepower, and 525lb-ft

(8277cc, 372kW, 712Nm). The new engine was both more powerful and lighter; and it produced 90% of its peak torque from 1500 to 5600rpm (redline stayed at 6000rpm). Finishing off the gains, one year after launch, it passed Low Emissions Vehicle (LEV) requirements.

The car came out more than ten years after the original, and other automakers had been catching up. Team Viper therefore set their sights on the number 500, going one step beyond the original's 488 cubic inches, 400 horsepower, and 450+ pound-feet of torque.

To reach 505ci, Team Viper increased both the bore and stroke – from 4.00x3.88in to 4.03x3.96in (101.6x98.5mm to 102.4x100.6mm). The wider bore was facilitated by a new cast-aluminum block, with interference-fit cast iron liners and cross-bolted main bearing caps; the external dimensions were unchanged.

The new pistons were cast from an aluminum alloy and tapered to reduce weight; new cracked-steel connecting rods were lighter but stronger than past rods. Both the block and heads were made of sand-cast, thin-wall, semi-permanent mold (SPM) 356 T6 aluminum alloy; cast iron cylinder liners were thermally inserted into the block.

Working with computer flow models, engineers improved the performance of the intake and exhaust ports, as well as combustion chamber cooling and sealing. The die-cast magnesium valve covers were lower-profile and incorporated steel internal baffles and anti-slosh foam. A multi-layer steel (MLS) gasket helped with sealing between the head and block.

The 2003 Vipers used hybrid organic additive technology (HOAT) coolant to reduce maintenance costs. A new hydraulic cooling fan used residual fluid pressure from the power steering pump – an interesting approach; the computer controlled its speed with a pulse-width modified solenoid. A unique thermostat, rated at 185°F (85°C), had a sliding-sleeve design for gradual opening.

Can you stuff a Viper engine behind the back seat? Jim Sayen's team did, with this mockup Viper designed to show whether the car would still fit within the same 'hard points,' how many parts would carry over, how much extra a mid-engined design would cost, and whether there would be problematic tradeoffs. (Courtesy FCA US)

The camshaft was made of post-hardened ductile iron, and rode directly on the block, without cam bearings. The engine still had two valves per cylinder with roller-type hydraulic lifters, but with completely new parts to cut weight and reduce friction; some of the measures taken were using single-valve springs, larger-diameter intake valves, and new roller rocker assemblies. The timing drive looked the same as the original one but had no shared parts, and the timing chain, cam sprocket, and crank sprocket were all matched by the supplier, BorgWarner, before arrival at the plant. The engine was an interference design (if the timing chain broke, so did the valves).

The two intake plenums were cast together, as part of a single-piece cast aluminum intake manifold with shorter runners. That, along with a non-staged, two-barrel throttle body, helped lower the hood. The intake manifold integrated air and fuel delivery with tubular fuel rails, fuel injectors, sensors, wiring, and the throttle body, all delivered to the plant as one pre-tested unit.

At the other end, the exhaust was made of fabricated tubular stainless steel (1.625in/41.28mm diameter) with tri-Y manifolds; each manifold was close-coupled to a 1L catalyst, with secondary 1L door-sill catalysts and resonators. Dual crossover pipes had a crossover in the middle, ending at the side exits.

Other changes included a new oil cooler, updated engine cooling, and a revised air cleaner assembly with dual oval air filter elements; and a new power steering pump and pulley. The forged steel crankshaft, fully counterweighted, had 7.6cm main journals and 5.4cm rod journals; the mains were cross-drilled for lubrication. To get power to the ground more effectively, Dodge switched to the newly developed Dana 44-4 Hydra-Lok speed-sensing limited-slip differentials, with the same ratio and a spread bearing design.

The engine was clearly an evolution, despite its new outward appearance. It kept its cast iron liners, firing order, odd timing, 9.6:1 compression, 6000rpm redline, and bore spacing. A new premium fuel requirement required higher octane, moving from US-spec 91 to 93.

Dodge now recommended using Mobil 1 synthetic (10W30 weight), which was the factory fill; fortunately, it took less oil, but unfortunately, it still used 10.5qt (9.9L). Lubrication had always a challenge for a car with superb cornering; a new wet sump oil system with twin cast-in wing tanks addressed that. The bottom of the pan was brought 0.75in (19mm) closer to the crank centerline, so the engine could be lowered to improve stability.

The engine computer was still a JTEC (Jeep/Truck) design, with two 8-bit processors, one 16-bit processor, and an adaptive memory. The old fuel-injection linkage was replaced by a new single-cable system, to keep the twin throttle bodies synchronized and to reduce tip-in.

The most visible change from outside the car was a return to the side exhaust pipes; oxygen-sensor technology had improved enough to make that possible. Electronic mufflers with active noise cancellation reduced both back pressure and noise alike; to further reduce back pressure, the Viper had not two but four catalytic converters.

The Tremec (née BorgWarner) transmission got some love, too, with a short-throw shifter, single-piece main shaft, and new heat treatment for internal components. What's more, torque-handling upgrades from the GTS-R program were moved to the standard version. The 2003 Viper also used a 66mm longer tubular aluminum propeller shaft than the previous models. Gear ratios were the same as in the first models, both inside the gearbox and at the differential.

SMALL CHANGES BECOME BIG CHANGES

The 2002 press release claimed that the 2003 Viper started "as a simple plan to alter the RT/10's roofline," which "quickly grew to a 'blue-sky' redesign when designers and engineers discovered that the accompanying 2.6-inch

The team preserved much of the Viper look, which Jim Sayen later regretted since many thought the mid-engined Viper was a prototype rather than an engineering-and-costs mockup. One can't help but think this car would have appealed to buyers 'as is,' even with a cramped passenger seat and complicated driveline. (Courtesy FCA US)

[66.0mm] lengthening of the wheelbase would change more than 50 per cent of the car's body panels and many chassis components."

That seems a bit unrealistic, so we looked at a statement from John Fernandez, who now headed the "SVE" (Specialty Vehicle Engineering) team under which Team Viper operated. He reported that they had started looking at options for the next-generation Dodge Viper back in 1997. The main question was how to keep the car's fundamental nature intact; did they want to go Hemi V8, for example? Should they go to luxury?

The team decided to stick to an $85,000 price range, to pay for added modeling time, more lightweight materials, and, oh, yes, a real convertible hardtop. How much more expensive was a 2003 Viper than the 1992 RT/10? According to the US Bureau of Labor Statistics, just adjusting for inflation would bring the original $50,000 price up to $64,000 in 2003.

As for the convertible top, it was not powered; occupants moved the roof from its resting place to the windshield and back, and fastened or unfastened a single clamp holding it to the top of the windshield frame. The two-seater design made that easy to do. The convertible's integral folding top had a magnesium shell to cut weight, and replaced both the old fabric top and the old hard top. Chances are, that was faster, lighter, and more reliable than a power top would have been. Not only was the car now a convertible rather than a roadster, but it was a convertible with glass side and rear windows, and even an electric defroster.

The full-width sport bar was replaced by vinyl-covered, frame-mounted aluminum 'sport hoops;' and the single-piece, sheet-molded composite clamshell hood and front fenders, which some owners had complained about, was replaced by a more conventional SMC hood with resin injection molded fenders.

STYLING, DESIGN, AND AIRFLOW

The 1992 and 1996 Dodge Vipers had been developed under Tom Gale; the 2003 was started under Gale and finished under Trevor Creed following Gale's retirement. It started with sketches from numerous designers; six sketches were chosen to be turned into scale models, around two weeks after the assignment; the models were given to Gale and Creed, who chose two of them to be made into full-size clay and fiberglass models.

Gale and Creed had to choose between an evolutionary look and one which was a radical departure from it; they chose evolution, with a design from Osam Shikadu.

Shikadu had joined Chrysler in 1994, and had worked on the Chrysler Chronos and Citadel concepts. His 2000 Viper GTS/R concept was a coupe with a fuel cell and other racing gear, unveiled after he had been chosen to lead exterior design for the 2003 Viper.

Shikado said that he kept the lines of the original car, but with some more sophistication: "When I look at the original Viper, the most important design cues are the two massive elements which interlocked at the middle of the body. The original Viper has distinctive characteristics, but from some angles it looks cartoonish. I added some crease lines on the body surface; it is the strongest departure from the very rounded original. My intention was to make it appear to have been sculpted out of solid metal, representing strength and power."

Louvers were added to increase engine bay airflow, while the wheelbase was increased to enlarge the doors for easier entry and exit. The higher belt line, which was a definite Daimler-era trend, was intended to provide a stronger profile. Shikadu added, "I like the three-quarter view. It looks like some kind of predator set to capture the prey."

The original Viper's styling and design had been inspired by the AC Cobra and other sports cars; the new 2003 Viper was likely inspired by the 1992 Viper itself. There were some major changes, though, including dropping the old roadster's targa setup (with a fixed roof behind the driver), and using a new Viper emblem, facing forward on the hood.

The original project leaders, Bob Lutz and Roy Sjoberg, essentially said they felt the new design was pleasant, but less brash and bold; one problem of resolving compromises was that some of the character of the car would be lost, bringing it a step closer to the Corvette. On the other hand, that V10, with its seemingly boundless torque, kept the Viper in a class of its own, and the improvements to handling and acceleration couldn't be argued with.

It's possible that some of the styling changes were the result of wind-tunnel testing. The 1992 car looked like it would slip easily through the wind but did not, partly so it could stay true to the dimensions of the concept. The team dramatically cut wind resistance while increasing downforce in the coupe, but they still tried to maintain the look of the 1989 concept as much as they could.

There was more time now for the wind tunnel, more computer modeling on more powerful computers, and no demand to keep to the original. Air had to be diverted to cool the brakes, cool and feed the engine, while the car had to slip through the air and maintain downforce over the tires (but not so much as to wear them out before the race was over). Designers worked for many hours with $\frac{3}{8}$-scale and full-scale wind tunnels, particularly on the floorpan and rear decklid height; they also had to tune the rear spoiler and rear diffuser.

The GTS had used McLaren's rolling-floor wind tunnel; the SRT-10 used one in Stuttgart owned by the Forschungsinstitut für Kraftfahrwesen und Fahrzeugmotoren Stuttgart (FKFS), a private nonprofit group. Rolling wind tunnels use a moving belt to allow accurate measurements of airflow under the body; one

Some members of the mid-engined Viper team at a 2014 reunion. From left to right: Karl Schuneman, David Raffin, Craig Belmonte, Bob Soraka, Dick Winkles, John Donato, François Castaing, James Sayen, and Jean Russell. Dick Winkles wasn't on the mid-engined team, but he brought the Viper for the photo shoot, and was later put in charge of V10 engine development. (Courtesy Marc Rozman)

result of that was a full belly pan (2mm thick), starting just behind the engine and continuing to the rear fascia. The front of the body required little tuning, with its short overhang and tightly packaged headlamps. The rear was another story; the rear fenders, decklid, and fascia needed work to cut drag and increase rear-wheel downforce.

Ralph Gilles had joined Chrysler in 1992, and had worked on the interiors of the Intrepid ESX2, Jeepster, GTS/R, and Liberty concepts; he was now in charge of the Viper's interior, and became Chrysler Group's Director of Design and Product Identification in 2001. His goal was to put the driver first, which is why he moved the tachometer up front and center, making it larger than the other gauges. For the press release, Gilles said, "The tachometer is the only thing that most performance-oriented people care about. On the track, the rest – such as the speed – is irrelevant. With this much power on tap, revs are very important." The line of small gauges on the top-center of the dash were now in a vertical line on the left side of the center stack, where they would be more accessible.

The carbon-fiber surface on the steering wheel leather, taken from the 1999 Charger concept, was credited to Margaret Hackstedde, the head of color, fabric, and mastering design. Gilles said it was one of a "myriad little design elements that surprise and delight. You'll sit in your new Viper and say 'Wow, look at that. Someone really thought about that.'"

Gilles himself was a little surprised that they were able to keep the starter button from the 2000 GTS/R concept. He said, "People kept asking, 'You're not really going to do

that, are you?' … We just never took it out. Lo and behold, it got engineered and it's there. That was fun." It was fun, it worked, and it was practical enough.

Gilles said he wanted a straightforward design with basic shapes. To get there, he used metal, including a die-cast metal piece around the shifter, metal door-pulls, and exposed hardware which had, over the years, essentially left cars' interiors (Jeep actually used some faux fasteners). Gilles said, "It has been a dream of our team to put exposed precision fasteners in a vehicle. We're glad we got to do it in this new Viper. They are all functional. Every single one of them is actually attached to something. They hold the bezel together. They are not molded-in plastic dummies."

Overall, Ralph Gilles said, the snug interior "makes you feel contained. You feel like you're very secure in there. You can't help but feel like this was built for you."

THE WISH LISTS
The official vision for the SRT-10, according to the press release, was to build a true convertible version of the RT/10; to refine the original design without losing its outrageous qualities; to raise the benchmark for performance; and to maintain the back-to-basics approach.

Owners wanted more power, better brakes, lower weight, a real convertible top, a dead pedal, and more comfort; but they wanted to keep the basics the same, and did not want frills such as cruise control, digital instruments, traction control, and cupholders. They also wanted the styling to stay unique.

Team Viper wanted better handling, particularly in transitions – the area that seemed to get naïve owners into the most trouble. Typically, in a mass-production, mainstream car, the driver will hear screeching tires or feel sliding before they lose control. A few cars have been known for going straight from "feels great" to "why am I in this ditch?" – notably the original Volkswagen Rabbit GTI. The Viper gave some warning to very experienced drivers, but novices could easily cross the line without realizing it. In short, the design team wanted the driver to hear or feel a loss of control early enough to stay out of trouble. It is not easy to get the perfect transition states, especially without reducing cornering. (The press release referred to the change as "revised geometry for greater limit-handling progressivity.")

Team Viper also reduced diving on hard braking, and squatting on hard acceleration. Michelin provided yet another brand new tire design, using both new materials and new construction; the size was P275/35ZR18 in front and P345/30ZR19 in back. All four wheels were forged aluminum-alloy; the tires had air pressure sensors in the valve stems, and were a run-flat design so they could skip having a spare wheel and jack, saving both weight and money (though run-flats, popular at the time on sports cars, had their own disadvantages).

Chrysler Corporation had said over and over in its 1990s ads that it made handling better by pushing the wheels to the corners of the car, cutting the overhang; with this generation, Team Viper took that to heart. While the new 2013 Dodge Viper SRT-10 was 1.1in (27.9mm) shorter than the 1992-2012 models (175.5in, or 445.8cm), the wheelbase was actually longer by 2.6in (66.0mm), at 98.8in (251.0cm). The extra wheelbase was used to make it easier to get in and out, and to provide storage space for the convertible top.

The suspension architecture was similar to the prior model; it had lightweight cast aluminum unequal-length upper and lower A-arms, aluminum knuckles, and rear coilover shocks (dampers). Both front and rear shocks had low pressure gas charges; there were still front and rear stabilizer bars and rear toe-control links. The Dana 44 limited-slip differential was upgraded to a newly developed Dana 44-4 Hydra-Lok torque-sensing limited-slip model, with a spread bearing design. The power-assisted rack and pinion steering dropped from a 16.7:1 ratio to 15.7:1.

There was a little controversy over the suspension; the US government investigated complaints by two owners (eventually, that grew to eight) who said the rear suspension knuckle had failed, causing crashes. Both Chrysler and the government eventually found that the damage had been caused by the crash rather than the other way around, and that controversy faded away.

ENTER SRT

The 2003 Dodge Viper had a new designation, partly because Dodge had diluted the R/T badge over time. In muscle car days, R/T had meant clearly higher performance (well, technically, it meant 'Road/Track'); even in the early 1990s, the Spirit R/T was an impressive car, with 224hp (167kW) generated by a 2.2-liter engine in a relatively light body. After the Viper launched, though, buyers saw a Dodge Neon R/T that was just another trim level. Did that poison the well?

Dodge leaders could have changed existing R/T cars, but instead added a letter and took out a slash, creating SRT. SRT was defined as 'street and racing technology;' but maybe they started with 'Super-R/T' and fitted new words to the letters later.

The 2003 Dodge Viper SRT-10 was the first to carry the new name; some press releases still called it RT-10. The next SRT car, the SRT 4, was the fastest car sold for under $20,000, a new Neon boasting 215hp (160kW) from its turbocharged four-cylinder engine. The modified Neon did 0-60mph (0-97km/h) in just 5.6 seconds, with a V8-like 14.2 second quarter mile time, both quite good for the time. The 2004 SRT-4 had quarter-mile times below 14 seconds.

The next SRT cars were the 2005 Chrysler 300C SRT-8, Dodge Magnum SRT-8, and Chrysler Crossfire SRT-6. The 300C and Magnum shared a 6.1L 'Hemi' engine pushing out 425hp (317kW), beating the original Viper V10's power rating. Today, all SRT cars are Hemi V8s.

Dan Knott, director of SRT in 2004, proclaimed, "SRT delivers outrageous, head-turning vehicles to the enthusiast … team members must be able to make their own decisions and be held accountable for the results. The team needs to avoid bureaucracy, and move at light speed." Roy Sjoberg had set these as characteristics of Team Viper from the start.

SRT defended its purity; every SRT car at least matched the best in their class, and they went back to "outrageous" with their supercharged Hellcat cars (which in 2019 went up to an eye-opening 797hp, or 594kW, in the Dodge Challenger Redeye). The SRT crew always increased both straight-line performance and cornering ability; and when they could not meet their standards, they didn't produce a car at all, which was the fate of the planned 2013-16 Dodge Dart SRT.

What was the business case for this, in an era where everyone seems to be looking for ways to stick their name onto any irrelevant item they can, so they can milk their reputation? From Dodge motorsports chief Jim Julow: "We must differentiate ourselves based on performance and drivability in creating a true enthusiast car. We need these proof points because frankly, not everyone wants to have a 500-horsepower, two-door convertible. Not everyone necessarily wants to have a turbocharged, manual transmission small car. Not everybody's looking for an aluminum block full-size truck. But they're looking for a brand that's willing to put a little bit extra into everything it builds … "

Besides, as the old saying goes, what wins on Sunday sells on Monday; in modern times, where racing actual stock cars is not quite so popular among the general public, what grabs magazine covers in March sells in April. SRT established 'street cred' for Dodge, selling ordinary Neons, Intrepids, and Avengers (it didn't have much of an effect on the Chrysler brand itself). Just as the 426 Hemi engine in the 1960s lent credibility to lesser muscle cars and the ordinary cars on which they were all based, the Viper gave Dodge a definite aura, appearing on quite a few magazine covers and in other companies' ads for their own products.

STRUCTURE AND MATERIALS

Body rigidity helps cornering, but how to improve on an already rigid body without adding weight? Using aluminum or magnesium alloys would drive up costs too much; so Team Viper benchmarked best-in-class competitors and used iterative computer modeling. Lessons from the computer model would be incorporated into a new design, and tested in the computer, over and over. The Special Vehicles group had its own computer modeling team, which helped.

The new car used more carbon fiber, and had a massive magnesium-alloy structure for the dashboard (based on one in the Plymouth Prowler) which saved, depending on the press release, 28lb or 34lb (13kg or 15kg). The design

won an award for being the first to work with crash safety without steel parts. Engineer James Finck later commented, "One of the biggest challenges was just trying to innovate on these new lightweight technologies that hadn't been done before; we had to learn from the ground up."

The space frame had composite beams for safety; carbon fiber replaced heavier fender supports. Despite the weight savings, the frame's torsional frame stiffness increased by 31%, partly thanks to a new net-form-and-pierce manufacturing process.

Despite making the car wider and adding a real convertible top, designers and engineers cut around 100lb (45kg) from the weight of the 2002 Viper. The 2003 Viper SRT-10 weighed 3410lb (1546kg), impressive given its larger width and ever-increasing federal safety standards; that was around 66lb (31kg) lighter than the original's 3476lb (1577kg).

The lighter weight contributed to dropping 0-60mph (0-96.6km/h) times from 4.5 to below four seconds, with 0-100-0mph dropping below 13 seconds – a hefty improvement. Lighter weight gave stronger acceleration, faster braking, and better cornering.

OTHER CONCERNS

The problem of cabin heat was tackled head-on, aided by computer modeling of air distribution; a stronger, lighter

The GTS/R concept's tail was changed quite a bit, possibly for aerodynamic reasons. (Courtesy Marc Rozman)

air-conditioner compressor and redesigning the vents helped.

The steering wheel was moved so it faced the driver squarely, and the pedals re-aligned to the driver. How could they do what had been impossible? There were three answers: CATIA, more time, and a wide car – wider by a full 10in (25.4cm). The 2003 Viper was 84.8in (215.4cm) at its widest. That made the car more stable, as well as providing room for a straight-on steering column and properly aligned pedals.

The four-wheel antilock brakes kept the car in the lead in competitive comparisons (and saved a driver's life now and then); so did upgraded Brembo calipers (44/40 dual opposing pistons up front, and 42/38 dual opposing pistons in back, with 14-inch rotors at all four wheels). A remote-mounted Brembo parking brake joined the system. The stopping distance from 60mph (96.6km/h) was now a rather good at 'under 100ft' (30.5m).

Viper owners who complained about scraping the bottom of their car on their driveway had an extra ⅛in (3mm) or so of ground clearance – which was now listed as being 5.125in (130mm).

Leg and shoulder room were almost exactly the same as before, despite the shorter length and much greater width; but drivers could push their seats back by 7.6in (192mm), an improvement over the old 6.0in (152mm),

and the seatbacks could now recline through a 45° range rather than just 11°. The power-adjustable pedals remained, with 4in (102mm) of travel; since appearing on the Viper, they had been adopted by minivans, pickup trucks, and sedans. The driver foot rest (dead pedal) could be adjusted, too.

The 7000rpm tachometer may have seemed like overkill for a car rated to just 6000rpm, with a fuel cutoff at 6200rpm; it included an upshift and redline indicator arrow lamp. The 220mph (355km/h) speedometer on US-sale cars reflected some owners' addition of forced induction. The center stack had gauges for oil pressure, oil temperature, coolant temperature, and voltage, along with the red pushbutton starter. Warning lamps duplicated the gauges in some cases, but also covered open and unlocked doors, low tires, seatbelts, brakes, deck lid status, airbag status, high beams, ABS, fog lights, engine issues, turn signals, and whether the passenger airbag was off. A new three-spoke, leather-wrapped steering wheel had a 'carbon fiber look' and Viper medallion.

Aerodynamics likely dictated a switch to low-profile, flat windshield wiper blades, along with the lower hood.

In a trick borrowed from Mercedes, the side windows lowered themselves slightly when a door was opened, and raised themselves when closed again. Another minor change was battery run-down protection, which shut

The 2000 GTS/R concept at Eyes on Design. (Courtesy Marc Rozman)

David Kimble's excellent cutaway illustration. (Courtesy FCA US)

Look at where we came from, and it's clear where we're going. This race-inspired Viper concept is a finely tuned instrument, eager to deliver a virtuoso performance. Its cockpit features indispensable race track instrumentation within twenty-first century comfort.

VIPER GTSR

Move at the speed of thought, and you're bound to make waves. For Viper, those waves began in 1997, as black-and-white checkered flags acknowledged yet another victory. Now, this stunning concept vehicle takes Dodge's collected GTSR experience gleaned from the world's toughest courses, and applies it to what might be the next generation of the world's most respected production race cars. The result: an exceptional offspring born very much on the right side of the track — the finish line.

Dodge Viper GTSR Concept

Talk about an extraordinary track record.

Note an exterior sculpted to convey accomplished power, with lowered hood grille openings, and a unique spoiler system. Considering that Viper's wins stretch from Le Mans in France to the Petit Le Mans in Atlanta, it's clear this concept vehicle is one good idea whose time has come.

Dodge advertised the GTS/R concept to publicize its racing wins. (Courtesy FCA US)

'Fangs' had a resemblance to Daffy Duck when viewed upside down. (Courtesy Marc Rozman)

on the seats), reading lamps, locking glove boxes, speed-sensitive power locks, 310-watt six-disc CD player with seven Alpine speakers, six-point restraint provisions, tilt-steering, power trunk release, and one-touch power windows. These were not the basic cars they had been ten years earlier.

The Viper had used special halogens, which provided more performance than ordinary headlights, but an absurdly fast car like the Viper needs all the visual help it could get. For that reason, it complemented the HID high and low beams with halogen bulbs for high-beam fill lighting.

Near the end of 2003, Dodge showed off the "Viper SRT-10 Carbon" concept car, with a carbon-fiber fixed roof and hood; the engine, with ten separate throttle bodies, was estimated at 625hp (466kW). The concept suggesting to some that a coupe was on the way – though it was some time off.

For 2004, Viper buyers got red Brembo calipers, trunk carpeting, a folding tonneau cover, and a white paint option. The 2005s added Viper Race Yellow and Copperhead Orange to the paint list and a new black-with-orange interior. For 2006, the new coupe was finally available, and Dodge celebrated with a special ten-year-anniversary-of-the-first-coupe package. Jon Brobst told its story:

"The 1996 blue and white scheme was going to be a one-year design only; that was part of the prestige of buying the '96. They were going to build 2500 Indy Ram trucks to match it. However, because the '96 ran late (due to supply issues, mostly with wheels), they couldn't build the last 400 '96 cars, and if you don't have them built by December 31st, you can't call it a '96; it has to be a '97. Chrysler knew they weren't going to get all of their orders of the '96 GTSs built, so they had to carry over around 400 as '97s, but it was supposed to be a one-year color.

"They ended up making a single change to the stripe, so it didn't go through the license plate cell in the back; and the stripes were a little bit further apart (which was actually done to better align the pre-painted panels at the factory). A few dozen people canceled their blue and white carryovers, and there were a couple of lawsuits threatened and settled because they couldn't get their '96 pace car replicas and a '97 blue and white wasn't acceptable.

"Fast-forward ten years to the '06 coupe, and they want to do blue and white again; so they actually went to the records, found people who were original owners of

off accessories that were left on for a long time if the engine was not running. New electromechanical door handles were flush-mounted. Under the hood, owners could find new sensors and a new engine computer, with a 136-amp alternator, 2.0kW starter motor, and 600-amp battery.

Federal safety rules had advanced, so the new car had a child seat anchor system, front and rear multi-stage airbags, knee-blocker airbags, and three-point seatbelts with pretensioners, load limiters, and traveling inboard buckles. The car also came with an alarm, and 2.5mph (4km/h) bumpers in the US or 5mph (8km/h) bumpers in Canada. For convenience, Vipers had a full-length floor console with a soft-touch padded armrest, a covered storage bin with a mat inside to prevent rattles, CD storage, a cigar lighter, and an airbag shutoff switch. Numerous trim parts had satin chrome to avoid the direct sunlight reflections that normal chrome would bring.

IN PRODUCTION

Dodge showed off its new Viper at the usual Detroit auto show, but it was more fun to see it at Arizona's Luke Air Force Base airshow. Dodge competed with the Air Force, which entered its F-16 Fighting Falcon, nicknamed 'Viper,' in a half-mile race. The F-16, with its 1300mph (2092km/h) top speed, would probably win a longer road race, especially with its 9g turning capability; but it lost the half-mile challenge to the Viper SRT-10. The Viper Club of America raised over $25,000 for the base's morale and welfare fund in that event.

In 2003, the Viper car's only options were colors (red, black, and bright silver metallic); every car had the defroster, tinted glass, high-intensity discharge (HID) headlights, power mirrors, hard-roof convertible top, air-conditioner, dead-pedal, leather trim (suede and leather

Dodge Viper outracing an F-16. (Courtesy Jon Brobst, who took this photo from the taxiway)

blue and white cars in '96 who still had them registered, and called to say, 'We're thinking of making an '06 blue and white first edition coupe to commemorate the '96 blue and white. How would you feel about that, since you were told it would be a first year exclusive?'

"When they called me, I said, 'If you're commemorating the ten year old car with a tribute car, it's going to only enhance the value of the original '96, so I don't have a problem. You've got my permission if you need permission.' Then I joked, 'I got the first '96 back there in the factory in a ceremony. It was the first factory delivery. It was my honor and privilege. It was signed by all 86 people that built it on June 8th, 1996. I got the first GTS. If you want to repeat that ceremony, just for fun, ten years later, I'll buy the first one of the '06 coupes.' I was just joking, but he said, 'If you're serious, that'd be pretty neat. Let me look into that.'"

A few weeks later, Dodge called Brobst and asked if he was serious; and he said, "If you want to re-enact that neat ceremony where you had Dom Pérignon champagne and birthday cake to launch the car, if you want to redo it, I'll redo it." Thus, Brobst agreed to lay out $67,000 for the car, and Dodge invited him out to the factory. The head of Team Viper and Dodge design, Ralph Gilles, autographed the engine and drove the Viper off the assembly line. Then Brobst and his partner drove the car home from Michigan, just like he had back in 1996, stopping at Roanoke Dodge in Illinois just to duplicate the trip.

Sales were good, given that there was only one body style until 2006: they made 1875 cars for 2003, 2435 cars for 2004, and 2010 cars for 2005. When the coupe finally arrived in 2006, the company made 752 roadsters and 1117 coupes, a total of 1869 cars.

COMPETITION COUPE

A coupe was needed for racing, especially since the Corvette had followed the snake to Le Mans. The Viper had more horsepower, more torque, faster acceleration, better cornering, and a top speed of 190mph (306km/h), but no fixed roof; making the car slip through the air yet have optimal downforce would be quite a challenge.

The Viper Competition Coupe was announced the day the SRT-10 convertible was unveiled, "to create a racing car for Viper owners, strengthen the performance image for the Dodge brand, create awareness of the Performance Vehicle Operations group, continue Viper's road racing heritage, and maximize use of existing SRT-10 parts to minimize cost."

What was this Performance Vehicle Operations Group? It replaced Specialty Vehicle Engineering, and would be replaced by SRT; Team Viper continued throughout these changes.

Viper Competition Coupe production was estimated at 25 cars in the first year; the group planned to provide technical support for competitors at all events, and possibly provide parts through the Mopar aftermarket division. The Competition Coupe was eligible for racing in the Grand American Cup (Grand Sports Class) and SPEED World Challenge, but it wasn't street-legal, so it followed in the GTS-R's footsteps. Buyers interested in testing their mettle against other Viper owners could do so in the Skip Thomas Viper Racing League.

The body was a custom design based on the SRT-10, using carbon fiber and Kevlar. Dash panels were made of carbon fiber, and the rear window was Lexan. Dodge sold it for a little over $100,000, including a window net, driver-activated fire suppression system with electrical cutoff, Team Tech six-point restraint, differential cooler, ducted brakes, and a 26.4gal (100L) fuel cell. The standard safety cage was FIA certified, braced to the frame itself and including engine bracing; there was no passenger seat, just a single Racetech competition seat. Aerodynamically, the exterior had a front splitter, larger rear diffuser, partial undertray, and adjustable rear wing.

The V10 was rated at 520hp (387kW) and 540lb-ft (732Nm), thanks to a revised cam and exhaust; the compression ratio was the same as the stock car, but redline came at 6100rpm instead of 6000rpm. Other track tricks included better driver and engine cooling, a trap-door oil pan, lower-restriction racing mufflers, a lighter (lower capacity) battery, and a low-inertia flywheel; they ran on 93 octane fuel. The transmission and final drive were shared with regular production cars.

Driver and car setup performance can both be improved with data analytics, so Dodge included a Motec dash and data acquisition system with an ECU interface.

Herb Helbig with two Vipers after the airshow race.
(Courtesy Jon Brobst)

The double-wishbone suspension had spherical bearing control arm attachments, Moton monotube two-way-adjustable coilover shock absorbers (dampers), 2.25in (57.15mm) racing springs and a blade-type rear anti-roll bar which could be adjusted by the driver. The wheels were three-piece units, 18 inches front and rear – 13 inches wide in back, as usual, but 11in (28cm) wide in front. The six-lug production hubs were kept for the race version; so was the steering column, though a GTS-R type steering wheel was swapped in.

Tires were described differently in two press releases, with one claiming Michelin P315/30ZR18 and P335/30ZR18 racing slicks, and another citing Hoosier P305/645ZR18 and P345/690ZR18 racing slicks. The track of the Competition Coupe was wider than that of the SRT-10 roadster, by 5in (13cm) up front and over 2in (6cm) in back.

The quarter mile was reportedly achieved in 11.8sec at 123mph (198km/h), with a 192mph (309km/h) top speed, lateral acceleration of 1.25g, and 100mph-zero braking in 260ft (79m).

The body was dropped by around 2in

Herb Helbig with Luke Air Force Base commander Brigadier General Stephen T Sargeant.
(Courtesy Jon Brobst)

(5cm) so there was just 3in (7.6cm) of ground clearance; the drag coefficient was 0.40, with some wind resistance traded for downforce. Dry of fluids, the Competition Coupe weighed 2995lb (1359kg) with a 50/50 weight ratio (no dry weight was reported for the SRT10, but the curb weight, including all fluids, was 3357lb, or 1526kg). The racing car was also nearly 9in (22cm) longer than the production version, and a bit under 6in (15cm) narrower.

Production started with a price of roughly $100,000; by 2005, the price had risen to just over $130,000.

RETURN OF THE STREETABLE COUPE

For 2006 there were once again three Vipers, the Dodge Viper SRT10 Convertible, Dodge Viper SRT10 Coupe, and Dodge Viper Competition Coupe (the hyphen was dropped from 'SRT 10'). The company made 752 convertibles and 1117 coupes.

The SRT10 Coupe easily beat the Convertible's 0-100-0 time, dropping it down into "the mid-12-second range," according to Dodge. It kept the 'double-bubble' roof and wraparound taillamps of the GTS, along with the initial paint scheme – blue with white stripes.

For higher downforce and high-speed stability, the coupe had a sloping roofline and deck-lid spoiler. The front fascia, front fenders, hood, and doors were shared with the convertible; the side glass, rear fascia, rear quarter panels, and taillights were not. To make life easier for customers, the deck-lid was held open by gas struts, and the cargo area had a low lift-over. Convertible cargo space was just 2.25 cubic feet, or 63.7L; coupe owners got a far more generous 6.25 cubic feet, or 177L.

For 2006, the convertibles were sold in blue, red, black, yellow, and slate crystal (dark gray); coupe owners could also specify yellow, white, or orange. Either way, buyers could opt for the usual dual stripes, in black or bright silver, depending on their paint color (blue with stripes was a coupe-only option). As if to celebrate the arrival of the coupe, though, the company provided two forged aluminum wheel options: a five-spoke wheel and an 'H-spoke' wheel (other than color, this was the only Viper option). Satellite radio also became optional on both SRT10s.

The 2006 McLaren Diamondback Viper was an interesting variation; it was built by ASC, which also made Viper body parts for Dodge. The concept showcased carbon fiber body panels which cut 85lb (39kg) off the Viper's weight. It was coupled with a McLaren-tuned engine that made 615hp (459kW), using ten trumpeted air intakes, and a lowered suspension. Onlookers could have been forgiven for thinking it was a prototype of the 2007s.

THE VIPER EXPERIENCE

The company had a series of ride-and-drives across the country; a well-known professional driver took people out in 'America's supercar' as part of the event. (Dodge reportedly let people drive for themselves until one guy drove off in

(Courtesy Marc Rozman)

the car; he was caught a few blocks away, and didn't try to run, so maybe he just misunderstood the program.)

Before they even got into the car, the test driver told passengers to watch for the hot door sills, which would "fry your skin quicker than a chicken leg at KFC!" – people could forget to watch their legs once, but not twice. The seat bolster kept passengers firmly in place, making it a bit hard to shift weight; it was best to get in right the first time. The convertible roof cut off the rear-passenger side view when up, which is hardly unusual in convertibles; the rear view wasn't generous, either, with the top up.

Starting up was a two-step process: turn the key in the ignition, then press the big red start button. At that point turning on the air-conditioning was also a good idea, because the V10 heat comes in through the firewall, the door sills (from the exhaust underneath), and even from the center console.

The clutch was praised for its lightness; drivers of older sports cars may have expected something far heavier, but the Viper clutch and torque made it easy to drive smoothly. Indeed, with the massive torque, one problem of turbo engines and older, carbureted motors – hesitation (from turbo lag or, for the older cars, "bogging" when fuel flooded the cylinders) – wasn't an issue. Many sporty cars tended to have most of their power at higher engine speeds, so if the driver suddenly hit the gas, but

wasn't in a low enough gear, they wouldn't react quickly; the Viper had plenty of "go" right off idle speeds. The ride was hard, but not as punishing as some other, less capable cars; and the car was excellent around turns.

The torque made the car absurdly responsive. Blip the pedal slightly in neutral, and the tach responded instantly; blip the pedal when in gear, and the car responded instantly. The engine had a good linear power delivery, without surprises, making it surprisingly easy to drive smoothly, and also to suddenly change speeds if needed.

With the professional test driver in charge, the car revealed its other personality, pinning passengers into their seats with instant G-forces, like a rocket but with quicker punch off the line. A man who had experienced racing with Chrysler's legendary 426 Hemi and Super Stock 413 V8s described the Viper as being in a completely different category, launching harder than anything in his experience. It was brutal but launched straight and stayed under control; being in the hands of a pro driver was akin to one of the better roller coasters.

The next generation would start with the 2008 Dodge Viper SRT10. According to Jon Brobst, a 2007 model year had been planned; but when people heard about the "Gen 4" cars, purchases slowed, and a few people canceled their orders. There were no 2007s.

(Original photo courtesy Marc Rozman)

6
'More venom' for 2008

After the first Viper came out, Chrysler had moved its engineering center and headquarters from Highland Park to Auburn Hill, been acquired by Daimler-Benz, and sold to a private-equity firm. For a time, the entire Viper program was up for sale to the highest bidder.

Rumors started in 2007, when the company said it was closing the Conner Avenue plant where the Viper was made. Some thought Chrysler would outsource production to Magna or another contractor; but, with McLaren helping GM to make ever-more-powerful Corvettes, and the Hemi V8 giving Dodge's big cars more power, the business case for the Dodge supercar was not as strong as it had been.

In the midst of the rumors, budget-cutting, and corporate machinations, the team made some hefty improvements to the 2008 Dodge Viper. The convertible and coupe appeared at the same time; the bodies were largely carryovers. Most of the news was under the hood; Ricardo Consulting and McLaren Performance Technologies had been consulted on optimizing the big V10 (McLaren was also working with GM on the Corvette V8, in the same building).

The result was a big power boost for the 2008 Viper. The 500s were old news now; it was time to hit 600hp (450kW) and 560lb-ft (760Nm). They needed the boost just to get ahead of the new 505hp (377kW) Corvette Z06.

The redline was pushed up to 6250rpm, aided by new valve springs and a new cam; peak power now came in at 6100rpm, the old redline. Lifters were lightened by 28g each. The cylinders were bored out slightly more, from 4.03in (102.4mm) to 4.055in (103.0mm), raising displacement ever so slightly, from 8.3L (505ci) to 8.4L (510ci).

New heads, shaped by CNC machines, had been developed using computer flow models; their larger valves could pass 23% more air/fuel mixture and 12% more exhaust. Piston pins were larger and had bronze bushings; the forged powder-metal connecting rods were secured with aircraft-quality fasteners for better fatigue strength.

Iron cylinder liners once again pressed in; and the main bearing caps were cross-bolted for strength. The bulkheads were stronger and the water jackets afforded better cooling. A new cast-aluminum two-piece intake manifold had smoother runners (for airflow), bolted to an upper plenum, with a new airbox design that cut weight and increased flow.

The basic engine architecture was unchanged, but it had a higher compression ratio (10.2:1), and took another half-quart (0.4L) of oil; the cooling system required 3.2 more quarts (3.1L) of coolant. A larger oil pump, with a swinging oil pickup adapted from racing engines, helped at cornering and acceleration extremes.

Mechadyne cam-in-cam variable valve timing adjusted when exhaust valves opened and closed according to engine speed and load – just what Dodge needed to comply with California's Low Emissions Vehicle 2 mandate. This was the first time any high-performance cam-in-block engine had variable valve timing; and it improved the idle, widened the power band, and lowered emissions. The new cam profile had higher lift and longer duration than in the past. Rated fuel economy also increased, reaching 13mpg city, 22 highway (5.5km/L city, 9.4 highway), making this the most fuel-efficient Viper to date.

California also required misfire detection, a real challenge on a V10 with two different firing intervals; but they managed it.

Engine man Dick Winkles behind the wheel. (Courtesy Marc Rozman)

Dick Winkles' customized engine. (Courtesy Marc Rozman)

The exhaust used double-walled air-gap tubular headers to increase flow, and to light up the catalyst more quickly; the headers' stainless steel outer shell was a thermal shield for the individual runners. One long-awaited change to the exhaust was dropping the crossover (introduced in the 2003 models), which had made the cabin even hotter.

The new V10 design called for platinum-tipped sparkplugs, with one coil per cylinder mounted on the head covers (and, for appearance's sake, under cast covers); 'throttle by wire' used dual electronic throttle controls. A new control system, provided by Continental,

monitored the crank and cylinder positions up to six times during each spark; the computer, dubbed 'Venom,' had ten times as much processing power as the 2007 PCM, and ran on the CAN bus. The alternator went from 132 to 180 amps, its highest rating so far.

The torque would have overpowered the BorgWarner/ Tremec T56 transmission; fortunately, Tremec had a newer model, the TR6060, which used 10% wider gears to increase torque capacity; the gears themselves had machined teeth. The transmission also used triple synchronizers for first gear and double synchronizers for second through sixth. Overall, it required less effort

Engine signed by Dick Winkles, Herb Helbig, Graham Henckel, Ralph Gilles, and Mark Trostle. (Courtesy Marc Rozman)

to shift, and the shifter had less travel. Lubrication was handled by Mopar's own ATF+4 automatic transmission fluid, rather than Dexron III; owners were told to change it every 96,000mi or 160,000km. An aftermarket version of the transmission was later sold as the 'Tremec T-56 Magnum.'

Clutch effort was also reduced, by using a smaller, twin-disc setup (rather than the old single disc), which cut rotating inertia by 18%. The new clutch could handle more heat and torque alike. Finally, Team Viper made provisions for adding an external transmission cooler – though it wasn't installed, owners who raced could do so more easily.

GKN had developed a new limited-slip differential, the Visco Lok, which Team Viper adopted; it kept the Dana M44-4 rear axle. Wheel sizes and materials were unchanged, but buyers could choose between three styles (five-spoke, H-spoke, and 'Razor' with five U-shaped spokes). Brembo continued to supply brakes, with 44/40 calipers in front and 42/38 in back.

Run-flats had been adopted in the 2003 cars; now, Team Viper dropped the run-flats and switched to Pilot Sport PS2 tires with four grooves (P275/35ZR18 front, P345/30ZR19 rear). Drivers reported that they increased both grip and driver feedback, while making the ride smoother.

The suspension was also retuned, though the basic architecture was the same; the springs, anti-roll bars, and shock absorbers were all changed to make the cornering more neutral.

The main exterior changes were the wheels and a new hood with a larger scoop and louvers for better cooling. Dodge had no fewer than eight colors, five of which were new (Venom Red, Snakeskin Green, Viper Violet, Viper Orange, and Bright Blue); there were six optional stripe colors, too (white, black, silver, graphite, blue, and red). In 2010, that expanded to 12 colors with seven stripe options; the colors were white, red, silver, graphite (dark gray), black, 'Very Orange,' 'Toxic Orange,' yellow, 'Snakeskin Green' (a bright color), 'Anaconda Green' (a very dark green), GTS Blue, and Viper Blue Metallic. Stripes were white, black, bright silver, graphite metallic (dark gray), red, and blue; there was also an ACR stripe, black with a thin red sub-stripe around a fifth of the way in. ACR cars had unique wheels.

The roadster and coupe shared their front fascia, fenders, hoods, and doors. Though the Roadster (convertible) had a slight space increase in trunk space. Outward visibility from the coupe was quite good, other than a limit on the windshield height which may have caused some Viper drivers to stop far back from traffic lights.

The 2008-2010 Vipers kept the 2006 body components and convertible tops, which was good for Viper store PartsRack. The shop had bought around 200 bodies worth of parts from ASC during the supplier's 2007 bankruptcy, some meant for the cancelled 2007 Viper; others were 2006 parts, rejected for even minor flaws.

PartsRack had already registered with Chrysler to bid on surplus property, so it could register with the Court to bid at the ASC bankruptcy auction after paying a deposit ("earnest money"). For the final payoff, PartsRack had to bring in a stack of thousand-dollar money orders; if there were more parts than in the original estimate, it would hand over more money orders. PartsRack's Jon Brobst wrote, "The auction was boring, a sealed bid through the Court, but picking up the parts at a deserted factory was cool."

The pickup, at the shuttered ASC plant, took five semi trucks. The pre-painted parts were stored in felt-lined bags hung from parts racks; as PartsRack took out the panels, Saleen workers grabbed the racks, having won the painting contract. There were some jokes about PartsRack and parts racks; but it was a special event for the PartsRack team.

The interior was changed largely by adding four color combinations: black with red, black with blue, black with slate, and black with tan. Buyers could choose between 'light arc' and graphite instrument panel and console bezels.

The dashboard was unchanged, dominated by the tachometer; black-on-white gauges reported the speed, oil pressure and temperature, coolant temperature, and voltage. The red start button and ignition switch were unchanged. The convertibles top design was the same.

New safety features included pillars above the belt line and instrument panel to limit head-impact force; pretensioners distributed the force exerted onto seatbelts, then gradually released.

Almost everything was standard. Options included the Protection Group (a fitted car cover and embroidered floor mats), satellite radio, navigation, and a premium tan interior including Nappa leather seats with perforated centers for hot days. The Aero Appearance group added a narrow rear wing and a front splitter; and there were an unprecedented number of colors – nine for the Roadster and Coupe, and five for the ACR.

The Viper experience began when the driver pressed a release at the top of the door; that popped it open, eschewing a conventional door handle.. It seems a bit odd for a 'back to basics' car.

The seats had good thigh support and bolsters, with manual adjustments for fore/aft movement and, as with the '92s, electric pedal adjustment; the steering column also tilted. The pedals were still offset a little to the left, though not as far as in the original cars. The trunk still held no spare tire, despite the loss of the run-flats; owners with a flat would have to use the repair kit and compressor.

Reviewers noted that the Viper was still brutal under acceleration, shoving the driver back into the seat; sharp turns generated strong g-forces. First gear could take drivers from zero to highway speed, and any gas-pedal movement was quickly rewarded with a leap forward. Yet, the Viper could be driven gently, with the new clutch design helping drivers make smooth, quiet shifts. Lugging the engine wasn't much of a worry with the low-end torque, even in top gear.

The production car. (Courtesy Marc Rozman)

79

Body panels were placed in these racks for storage and transportation to the Viper plant. (Courtesy Jon Brobst)

From the left: Charlie Brown III, Doris Rose, Jon Brobst, Al Byerle, and Paul Scharf; Charlie Brown and Al Byerle were retired members of Team Viper. (Courtesy Jon Brobst)

As one would expect, the wheelbase, length, width, height, and ground clearance remained the same, but the fuel tank shrank from 18.5gal (70L) to 16.0 (60.6L); that weight-saving measure was justified by higher fuel economy. Weight was now listed as 3454lb (1567kg) for the coupe and 3441lb (1561kg) for the convertible, with a 49.6/50.4 weight distribution for both. The two cars also shared a coefficient of drag of 0.38 (0.42 with the top down on the Roadster).

The power boost shaved some time off the 0-60mph (0-97km/h) run, rated at 'under four seconds;' the quarter mile ('mid-11-second range'), and the 0-100-0 run, which could be run in 11 seconds flat.

UNVEILING AND SPECIAL EDITIONS
The 2008 Dodge Viper SRT10 was unveiled in Los Angeles in mid-2007. It was clearly an update of the 2003, but enough had changed to justify a 'fourth generation' tag.

The price, when it went on sale roughly a year later, was $83,145 for the convertible and $83,895 for the coupe in the United States, not including the gas-guzzler taxes. That was still a reasonable price, given that only a handful of street-legal cars came close to its performance; and the Viper was as well-made as any. The price also included the one-day SRT Track Experience

training program (in 2009, supplied by Richard Petty's organization) to build skills for street and track driving.

2008 Viper production showed the effect of the price increase: 712 convertibles, 688 coupes, and 179 ACRs, for a total of 1579 cars.

The PT Cruiser had boosted sales through limited-run 'special editions,' and this generation of the Viper used the same technique. Buyers could get a 1.33 Edition (in honor of a record lap), a Vooodoo Edition (reportedly based on Ralph Gilles' conference-table), a Canadian Edition, the Snakeskin Green ACR, three special dealer versions (one each for Woodhouse Dodge, Tomball Dodge, and Roanoke Dodge), and the Final Edition. Any dealer could sign up for the Dealer Exclusive Program – but only three did.

MEET THE NEW ACR AND COMPETITION COUPE
The Competition Coupe continued with the 2008s; it had a carbon-fiber Kevlar body, safety cage, window net, six-point restraint, fire suppression system, differential cooler, ducted brakes, and racing slicks. In 2010, that package cost roughly $200,000.

The ACR package restarted in 2008, after having been retired back in 2002; it now included StopTech slotted lightweight rotors, aerodynamic improvements, a racing suspension, and weight savings. The top speed was listed as 180mph (290km/h); the price was 'under $100,000' in

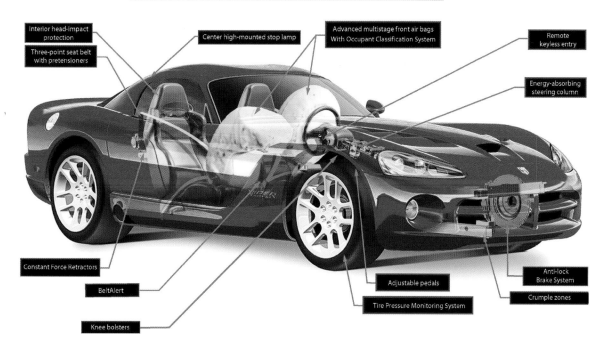

2008 DODGE VIPER SRT10 - Safety and Security Features

The Viper's safety features, nicely illustrated in this press graphic. (Courtesy FCA US)

2009, but the 2010 ACR listed at $108,785 as equipment was added in. Buyers had a choice of five colors (red, black, violet, blue, and orange) with an optional two-tone paint scheme that included a black hood, roof, decklid, and wide front fascia stripe, presaging other Dodges' 'Blacktop' editions.

The ACR aero package included a variable-geometry front splitter with three removable rub strips, an adjustable rear wing, and front dive planes; all had been developed in computer simulations and tested in wind tunnels. The splitter and dive planes were made of autoclaved carbon fiber for cut weight. To keep the wheels on the road, Team Viper chose KW Suspensions adjustable coilover racing dampers with two-way adjustable shocks. The wheels were forged aluminum Sidewinders with Pilot Sport Cup race/street tires. The aero, suspension, and tire choices brought the Viper ACR's cornering past 2.0G.

For those who were really serious about racing, or who had another car for street driving, Dodge offered an ACR Hard Core package. That went further in weight reduction, removing the stereo, air-conditioner, hood silencer, trunk carpet, and tire inflator; the radio was replaced by a lap timer mount (the lap timer came with the car), and the speaker holes in the door were covered by carbon-fiber panels. One source claimed that many Hard Core models were ordered by accident, with people thinking they were adding the radio and air-conditioning, rather than removing them. The Hard Core is still rare – air-conditioning was a hard option to remove.

The Viper ACR weighed in at 3408lb (which translates 1546kg, but Dodge claimed 1552kg). ACR Hard Core was listed as 3366lb (1527kg, or, as Dodge wrote, 1533kg). Thus, the ACR was 46lb (15kg) lighter than the Coupe; and the ACR Hard Core was 42lb (19kg) lighter than the ACR. (Chrysler's conversions between English and metric weights were incorrect for the ACR; but the company wrote that the ACR was over 40lb lighter than the normal coupe, so the English weights may have correct. It's also possible that the cars were actually weighed in kilograms, the conversions to pounds were incorrect, and the press release writer did their math in pounds.)

After testing at the Nürburgring track, SRT engineers adjusted the Tremec TR6060's fifth gear ratio, moving it from 0.77 to 0.796 for the 2010 ACR; the 2020s also had a shorter-throw shifter and an altered aerodynamic package which improved rear yaw and overall performance, increasing the top speed by 4mph (6km/h).

RACE-ONLY: VIPER ACR-X

Fifty race-only, not-street-legal Dodge Viper ACR-X cars

Opposite page, top: Inside Dick Winkles' personal car: the interior layout was carried over from the 2003-06 series.
Bottom: Dick Winkles' car at a 2014 gathering.
(Both courtesy Marc Rozman)

were built near the end of the run for use in the Viper Cup Series. Taking off some emissions gear, using a lower-restriction exhaust, swapping in long-tube headers added up to a 40hp (30kW) gain over the stock engine, with torque rising to 605lb-ft (820Nm).

Extra dive planes and other changes increased downforce by 100lb (45kg) at 150mph (241km/h); the standard Viper ACR had an already impressive 1100lb (499kg) of downforce at that speed. The suspension was retuned for on-track usage. Like the Competition Coupe, the car included a roll cage, fuel cell, and race seat.

Between stripping out the interior and using more lightweight materials, Team Viper got the weight down to around 3200lb (1451kg). Buyers had the usual dashboard and center console, but no moving side windows or a passenger seat, a removable Momo wheel (looking a little out of place), a fire suppression system, transmission and differential coolers, better front brake ducting, and larger front rotors.

The car had no warranty and cost $110,000, but it beat the Viper ACR's record at Laguna Seca by roughly three seconds, and lapped Nürburgring over nine seconds faster than the ACR. It was adapted from the usual Viper by Roush Racing in Livonia, Michigan.

Dodge Viper Cup races started in July 2010; the ACR-X was the only model in the series, which ran two races per weekend for five weekends in 2010. The contingency program paid out $200,000 in the first year, in cash and Mopar vouchers (the first place payout included $6500 in cash and $1000 in Mopar vouchers; fifth place was good for $500 in cash and $100 in vouchers). The top three series finishers had bigger stakes, with $25,000 going to the champion, $10,000 to the runner-up, and $5000 to the third place winner.

As the televised Viper Cup races went on, one or two 'social influencer' celebrities were invited to join each race, after some training. Jon Brobst and his partner, Doris Rose, drove pace cars for the series; Brobst later said, "Pace car duty for the Viper Racing League was the highlight of my career; it was all-Viper excitement on some of the best tracks."

SELLING THE VIPER, FACTORY AND ALL

Daimler had sold Chrysler to Cerberus Capital Management in August 2007, choosing the private equity firm over two groups that were perhaps better suited to the task: Kirk Kerkorian and a group of plant workers, and, more important, Canadian parts-maker and contract auto producer Magna. Cynics may have thought that Cerberus was the least likely to yield a long-term success story, which would embarrass Daimler.

The newly independent Chrysler was cause for celebration for many employees and owners, and Cerberus followed through by hiring highly regarded executives and talking about restoring an American icon. Many employees or facility managers joyfully painted over

Top: Dodge Viper ACR. Above: two Vipers on display at an Auburn Hills car show.
(Both courtesy Marc Rozman)

the word 'Daimler' on DaimlerChrysler signs or transport trucks. Outside of Team Viper, Daimler had not been good for Chrysler, which had been cut to a third its prior size. The morale boost disappeared when Cerberus hired its new CEO: Robert Nardelli, known for cheapening products with 'lowest possible cost' Chinese imports at Home Depot (which had paid him $210 million to leave before his contract was up).

Chrysler was shopped to buyers around the globe as Cerberus shifted parts suppliers to lowest-bid import and abandoned the Plymouth Road complex where Team Viper had started. With the 2008 bank failures, rumors of bankruptcy became self-fulfilling; outgoing President George W Bush provided hefty bridge loans so incoming President Barack Obama and the Canadian government could

organize a rescue of GM and Chrysler (Ford was on the edge, as well, surviving largely on credit and a massive interest-free government loan from the Department of Energy).

In August of 2008, Cerberus put the Viper plant and property rights up for sale. The Viper was still a world-beating car, and its parts were used by several exotic car companies; it seemed like a prize anyone would want. Alfa Romeo had made nine Zagato TZ3 Stradales, essentially Vipers with Alfa Romeo's own carbon-fiber body, but using the Viper chassis and interior (the body panels and wheels left over from the conversion were sold to the American Viper parts shop PartsRack).

The Spanish GTA Spano hit production in 2010, getting a movie cameo (*Need for Speed*, 2014) and game appearances (*Forza Horizon 3 and 4*); it used the Viper

Showing off at the Chrysler Employee Motorsports Assocation (CEMA)'s annual show on the Chrysler campus. (Courtesy Marc Rozman)

Shown at CEMA. (Courtesy Marc Rozman)

engine with a choice of manual or sequential automatic transmissions, and a carbon fiber and titanium chassis which cut weight to 2976lb (1350kg). Twin turbochargers pushed power to 769 or 829hp (574 or 618kW), making it a true supercar. The price, though, was a stunning €692,975.

Bristol was also a possible buyer, as it was still making the Bristol Fighter, a Viper-based car that ran from 2004 to 2011 with a choice of the manual or a four-speed automatic to go with its modified Viper engine. Bristol only made a few Fighters during those seven years, though; some sources claim 13, but Evo reported 46 sold by 2008, when it started at £235,000. In any case, Bristol didn't have the resources to buy the Viper operation.

Devon Motorworks, owned by Rent-A-Car Racing and ORECA racer Justin Bell, also seemed likely; the

Devon GTX was essentially a Viper with more carbon-fiber in the body, a revised intake and exhaust, a cast aluminum double-wishbone front and rear suspension, and aftermarket brakes. There would be two Viper-based cars later, one from Prefix Performance (just ten were made), and one from VLF, a company created by Gilbert Villareal, Bob Lutz, and Henrik Fisker. Again, though, Devon did not have the resources.

Congressman Darrell Issa claimed that Cars & Concepts owner Dave Draper and a group of investors had offered $35 million before the bankruptcy. Court documents claimed that, in the prior year, Dodge had only made 289 cars, but had generated a profit of $16 million including merchandising. It's possible that the bid was rejected as being too low; and there were no bids for the Viper plant during the bankruptcy itself.

Despite the bankruptcy, Team Viper was at work on a new generation; and once Fiat's CEO, Sergio Marchionne, came into the bankruptcy talks, the Viper was taken off the table. Was there room for hope?

On July 10, 2009, Chrysler made it official with a press release headed, "Dodge Viper SRT10 Will Live On." After a single paragraph restating the headline, the release read, "Originally slated to cease production in December 2009, the Chrysler Group Conner Avenue Assembly Plant – the exclusive home of Dodge Viper production since 1995 – will continue to build the V10 powered sports car. Chrysler Group is no longer pursuing a sale of the Viper business assets."

Dodge had made 25,000 Vipers since the 1992 launch (#25,000, built in March 2008, was presented to NASCAR driver Kurt Busch). Incoming Chrysler leader Sergio Marchionne had given owners another year of Viper production; but he hadn't committed to a new generation yet. With the Corvette and a Shelby Mustang both reaching 600hp with supercharged V8s, the Viper would need an update to stay viable.

THE 'FINAL' YEARS

The 2009 Viper had a revised center console bezel and recessed window switches; the frame, fuel tank, and filler were all modified as well. There were also new colors (Anaconda Green, Graphite Metallic, Diamond Black, and Viper Bright White), as well as the continuing Venom Red, bright orange, and bright blue; likewise, racing stripes were available in white, black, silver, graphite, red, blue, and orange.

Dodge released the buyer profile for the Viper when it launched the '09 series; 96% of buyers were male, with a median age of 45 years and an annual household

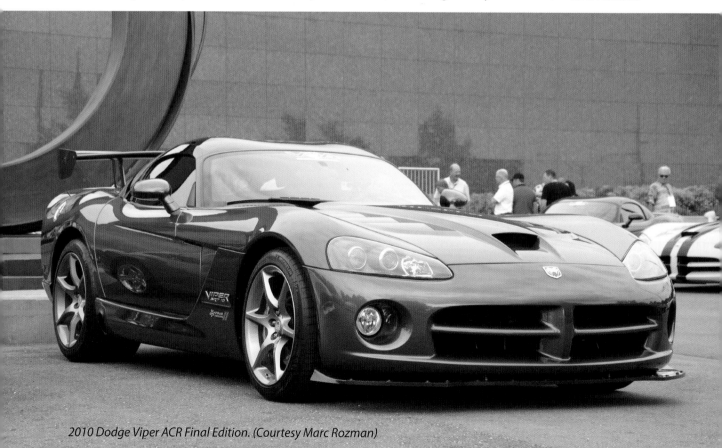

2010 Dodge Viper ACR Final Edition. (Courtesy Marc Rozman)

income of $173,000 (presumably a median). 44% of buyers were college graduates, and 62% were married. 2009 production was 167 Roadsters, 241 Coupes, and 245 ACRs.

In late 2009, Dodge leader Ralph Gilles announced that there would be no more Vipers after the summer of 2010. Fifty cars (20 coupes, 18 roadsters, and 12 ACRs) made up the Final Edition; they were available in the Coupe, Roadster, and ACR versions, with a silver-gray body and black center stripe, traced in red. The interior was black with red accents, with a numbered dash plaque and special floor mats. They all had six-spoke Anthracite-painted wheels, except the ACRs, which had black Sidewinders. The actual last car was not a Final Edition; it was more personal than that.

The last 'ZB' Dodge Viper rolled off the line on July 1, 2010. Viper Club of America and Motor City Viper Club members were invited to watch (400 showed up) as a

final car, customized for D'Ann Rauh, came down the line. Both the gold-with-orange-stripes paint scheme and the leather interior appointments were custom-designed by D'Ann and her husband; they had the world's largest Viper collection, owning 40 snakes. SRT's Bob Soroka airbrushed layouts of race tracks into the copper stripes.

The final car was the 28,061st produced; sales had wildly exceeded early expectations.

After the little factory celebration, the group traveled to the Walter P Chrysler Museum; some key people from the Viper program, including Tom Gale, were there, with 100 Vipers and 450 Viper owners, many of whom had flown in for the event.

Times were changing at Chrysler; under Sergio Marchionne's leadership, parts production was being brought back in-house, there were heavy investments in manufacturing, and new engineers were being hired to replace some of the thousands dismissed by Cerberus and Daimler. Perhaps a new Viper would be an outrageous way to change the dialogue about Dodge – just as it had been in 1989?

Viper ACR Final Edition on display at the Walter P Chrysler Museum.
(Courtesy Marc Rozman)

7

Surprise return: 2013-2017

MAKING THE CASE

Senior vice president in charge of design, Ralph Gilles, wanted to see the Viper return. The first step was giving the CEO, Sergio Marchionne, a key to one of the 2010 Vipers. The next step was showing him a video of the Viper breaking the record at the Nürburgring, and a list of the cars Dodge beat.

Gilles got people sketching, made a full size model, and took it to the Styling Dome – a large, quiet, perfectly lit area used for viewing models and cars. People started talking, and Marchionne said, "Be quiet! Let's just take this in."

Gilles made one last plea to save the car at an executive meeting; according to Maurice Liang, Sergio Marchionne turned to Olivier François and asked for his opinion. François said that the Viper added value to the company; and the majority of the board was in favor of resurrecting it.

The Viper's prior sales of 1500 cars per year were not sustainable because development costs had risen in the face of ever-more-capable competitors. Gilles estimated that they needed to sell 2500 cars per year, and could do that by providing more versions of it. They would also have to broaden their appeal outside of the current owner group, without destroying the essence of the car. The natural next step was finding out what owners of other exotic cars, such as Ferraris, Maseratis, Lamborghinis, Porsches, and high-end Corvettes wanted.

Dodge commissioned a study of high-end car owners and found that non-Viper-owners wanted modern features – traction control, cruise control, upscale interiors, and, yes, cup-holders. The non-owners, Gilles told *Car & Driver*, thought the Viper couldn't handle well, was too hot inside, and was badly made. The team decided to reconcile matters by having a hardcore version, which it dubbed the Venom (officially, the SRT), and a more refined version, dubbed the GTS (officially, the GTS).

The team made its proposal just a month after the final 2010 Viper was produced, and got the green light from Sergio Marchionne. We can see three plus-sides to the Viper program – boosting morale inside Chrysler; keeping Ralph Gilles, who was well-known and highly regarded by enthusiasts, and almost certainly being courted by GM and Ford; and keeping Dodge's credibility intact. Publicity was also a factor; Ralph Gilles even called in Maurice Liang, founding president of the Viper Club of America, to document SRT's development of the updated Viper. That resulted in a more detailed version of the development of the 2013 cars in Maurice's book *Viper: Return of America's Supercar.*

The old Plymouth Road (PROC) site been abandoned by the company, and now the SRT team had a suite on the top floor of the Chrysler Technical Center (CTC). Graham Henckel, who was in charge of engineering the new Viper, raced a Neon SRT-4 and owned a 2010 Viper. His main goals were to increase power, comfort, and refinement; cut weight; optimize gear ratios for both street and track; help the race program; and set a new record at Nürburgring for street-legal cars. They would also have to meet new safety and emissions rules.

While it would be cheapest, fastest, and easiest to keep the V10 and chassis, some wanted to start over or add newer technologies. The call went out to Ian Sharp of Flybrid Systems, a former Jeep and Lotus engineer with Formula One experience. Sharp recommended refining the car's design and building the race and production versions side by side, using sponsors to help foot the bill.

Sharp's most controversial suggestion was adding a flywheel-based kinetic energy recovery system (KERS). A Team Viper engineer found space on the front of the engine for the KERS shaft connection; the flywheel could be 'charged' at idle without a noticeable increase in fuel use. Overall, Flybrid Systems made three separate proposals over six months.

Whether it was seen as a vision that wouldn't play in Peoria, too long to implement, or perhaps one step too far, the 2013 Viper went along the path it had been following – more power, comfort, and customization – and the flybrid and other ideas went by the wayside.

Another road not taken was sharing with the Alfa Romeo 8C Competizione. The Alfa was too far from a Viper's dimensions, according to Mark Trostle; more to the point, they would have to move the engine too far forward, hurting the weight balance, and push it upwards to deal with the front suspension cradle (as Ralph Gilles told *Car & Driver*, "It would have stuck out of the hood.") Development time would end up being about the same.

Both McLaren and Ricardo had already tried to optimize the V10 engine. Rumors of 700hp (522kW) were floating around the internet; writing

Dodge showing off the new dashboard, with SRT Performance Pages, at an auto show. (Author)

Engine cutaway display. (Author)

Viper engine on display. (Author)

V10 Under a cross-brace. (Courtesy Jeremy White)

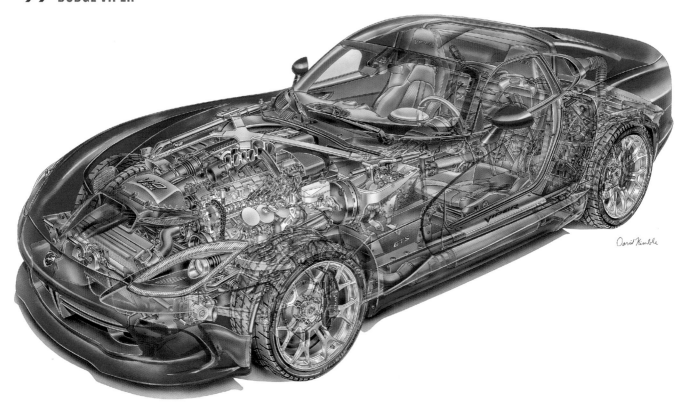

David Kimble's superb cutaway drawing. (Courtesy FCA US)

for enthusiast site Allpar, I predicted 640hp (477kW) on the assumption that the rumors reflected gross horsepower, not net, and knowing that it was enough to beat the supercharged Corvette ZR-1's 638hp (476kW).

The team looked at supercharging the big engine, which would definitely increase power; but there was little space for forced induction, and not enough time to develop a package even if they could deal with the heat. Team Viper had no desire to follow competitors whose cars had high peak power ratings, but couldn't maintain them on the track (indeed, the SRT team's later Hellcat cars stood out for maintaining their power over time).

Dick Winkles, head of the Viper's engine development, adopted an incremental approach, finding power wherever he could. The cam adopted a longer intake duration for more high-end power, the variable valve timing keeping emissions in check. Revised pushrods made it possible to find misfires, keeping US regulators at bay.

The air path was smoothed by using a composite intake (Chrysler's own 1995 Neon had been the first mass-produced car with one); that cut weight and smoothed the air path. Winkles' team improved the approach angle to the ports and lengthened the runners for more power at high revs. Dick Winkles claimed a 10hp and 20lb-ft gain (7.5kW and 27Nm) just from the new manifold, along with a 7lb (3kg) weight loss, and less heat transfer.

Using parts with greater heat tolerance, such as steel rings and sodium-filled exhaust valves (used by Dodge truck engines for decades) helped engineers to increase the rev limit to 6400rpm, while updated seals reduced engine friction. Forged Mahle pistons replaced the old castings, partly to withstand more heat, and partly because the cast pistons had caused problems for tuners who added forced induction.

Three technologies that didn't make the cut were direct injection, hemispherical heads, and overhead cams. There simply wasn't space for overhead cams or a "Hemi" design; and the wedge design made direct injection impractical. (paragraph) They kept the side pipes, but got better exhaust sound via new seals, engine mounts, and bushings.

In the end, Winkles' team was able to deliver 645hp (481kW) at 6200rpm, and 600lb-ft (814Nm) at 5000rpm; the fuel cutoff came at 6400rpm, but before that point, a red snake would light up on the tachometer as a warning. Fuel economy dropped a bit, to 12mpg city, 20 highway (5 and 8.5km/L).

Many owners had switched their stock 3.07:1 axle ratio for a 3.55:1 unit; Team Viper decided to use the customers' preference as a guide, moving to 3.55:1 for the axle, which meant they also had to change the gear ratios. Fourth remained direct drive, but all the other gears changed (the car could still go from 0-60mph, or 97km/h, in first gear).

Ralph Gilles introducing the Viper. (Courtesy Jeremy White)

The press kit: a small booklet and USB drive in a cylinder covered by a snakeskin wrap. (Author)

The tall sixth gear was brought down, cutting highway mileage ratings but giving more power to drivers in top gear. The shifter was revised again for shorter, lower-effort throws and rounded-off detents.

Using an aluminum flywheel cut some weight, so the Viper could use the power it had more efficiently; it was reportedly good for around a tenth of a second in the quarter mile. The engine was offset slightly towards the passenger, to balance side-to-side weight distribution

Inside the snake at its launch.
(Courtesy Jeremy White)

at the track; and changes to the block and head gaskets helped resolve an issue with high temperatures at the rear cylinders, which were causing the computer to slow timing in some cases.

Mark Trostle led the design end of the project, starting by creating a separate studio space (dubbed Area 51) to display dozens of sketches submitted from the studios. Six designs were made into ⅜-scale clay models. The designers kept refining their work, and eventually Scott Krugger's design was chosen for most of the car – with Tome Jovanoski's front end and portions of Alan Macey's work integrated into it.

For months after, Gilles sought ever-more-refined designs, helped by 3D-printed small-scale plastic models. Then he had a full-size clay made; Sergio Marchionne felt it was too close to the Viper GTS, and suggested replacing the fog lights with vertical LEDs, which were later replaced by vents. Gilles had a full-scale foam model made up with these changes to show

(continued on page 97)

SRT Viper on display. (Author)

It takes a Dodge to catch a Dodge. (Courtesy Marc Rozman, staged photos taken at a press event)

Time Attack. (Author)

Viper GTS .
(Courtesy Marc Rozman)

Carbon Edition. (Author)

Another Viper display car. (Courtesy Marc Rozman)

Carbon Edition. (Author)

Specially painted car illustrating the 2015 Viper GTC 'one-of-one' program. (Author)

2016 Dodge Viper ACR with Extreme Aero Package
Produces 1200+lbs of downforce at 150mph
Rear X-wing: Length: 1876mm, surface area: 8.08ft^2

2016 Dodge Viper ACR
Produces 1101lbs of downforce at 150mph
Rear X-wing: Length: 1776mm, surface area: 7.69ft^2

2016 Dodge Viper with TA 2.0 Package
Produces 400lbs of downforce at 150mph
Rear single element wing: Length: 1497mm, surface area: 4.98ft^2

Three aerodynamics packages. (Courtesy FCA US)

to the product approval committee, using wheels from the Grand Cherokee SRT8. A new Viper emblem, created by Viper owner and Chrysler designer Vince Galante, was later dubbed 'Stryker' based on suggestions from other owners. The body panels would be painted by Prefix this time around.

Other details were added over the months of development, some of which had to give way to airflow testing. The original headlights were reshaped using LED turn signals and daytime running lights (DRLs) to help get the desired shape.

As with the original, the team tried to use existing parts, including the past generation's mirrors, Lancia reverse lights, and Fiat 500 side markers. Chrysler already used 8.4in center screens and had 7in customizable gauges on the way for most of its cars, so the Viper could have these at a low cost – complete with programming. The Viper would leapfrog its more expensive competitors in that regard.

The customizable gauge cluster was the source of some argument; wasn't adding the big 8.4in-diameter center screen and a digital gauge cluster display exactly what Viper owners had said they didn't want, over and over again? They couldn't make two versions; it would add dramatically to the cost. In the end, both digital displays made the cut, partly because owners could use them to see their performance data and modify some aspects of their cars. The SRT Performance Pages recorded drivers' peak g-force, top speeds, acceleration times and such – and gave easy access to tuning for the suspension settings on the GTS ('street' and 'race').

Federal rules also required stability control systems and traction control now; they were anathema to Viper owners but the law was the law. Tuning the stability control was tricky, since it had to save the driver on snow, ice, rain, or even a dry surface where the driver miscalculated their traction; but it would have to stay out of the way most of the time, and let the driver be as aggressive as they wanted. It was a fine balancing act, though one that Jeep had been through in its own way – making a stability control system that allowed drivers to go off-road without a 'self-driving' feel.

The Viper's system would activate when absolutely necessary, and relinquish control quickly. In ordinary cars, it could be desirable to have the driver know traction control was on, and have it intervene quickly and stay on for a while; but the Viper was no ordinary car, and some owners would be looking for excuses to hate the 'nannybot.' They compromised by having four positions for the stability control, from full assist to completely off (to shut it off, an option not described in the manual, owners had to drive under 25mph while holding the button down for five seconds).

Pace car driver Jon Brobst was convinced; he later said, "The people who liked the no-bells, no-whistles approach raised an eyebrow and said, 'Do we really need all this stuff?' But I've bought a lot of wrecked Vipers and parts over the years; they were pretty hard to control. When I got behind the wheel of a 2013 Viper pace car for the first time, it was a very, very rainy race, and I was apprehensive, despite a lot of pace car and track experience. I live in the Pacific Northwest, so I've got a lot of experience driving Vipers in the rain, but I haven't had any track time testing it. I just put it on the street setting, and after one lap, the race control steward called me and said, 'Hey, pace car, slow down.' It really had great manners in the rain."

As long as stability control was in the cars, the team borrowed Launch Control and Hill Start Assist from the other Chrysler programs; they didn't add any weight, after all. Hill Start Assist applies the brakes when manual-transmission cars are on a hill, releasing them when the driver releases the clutch; it was in the company's cheapest cars as well as its most expensive (it was also used on cars with automatic transmissions). Launch Control was more of a racing tool: if the driver pushed a button on the steering wheel and held the revs to a certain point, the computer would, when the clutch was released, keep the throttle at the highest possible point without having the tires slip.

This generation wasn't just the first one with a digital dash and stability controls; it was also the first standard Viper to run without Michelin tires, switching to Pirelli P-Zero tires (P295/30ZR18 in front and P355/30ZR19 in back). They were reportedly far better in cold weather and snow (though Pirelli did not recommend using them in the snow; they were 'summer tires'). Pirelli P-Zero Corsas were optional.

The close relationship between design and engineering at Team Viper helped in many ways. Heat build-up in the headlamps required the group to move the lenses; at the same time, higher than expected drag in the wind tunnel required a front redesign, so the two problems could be dealt with at once. Likewise, the spoiler and air diffuser had to be moved to help with airflow and downforce, and the designers helped to keep the appearance intact. The hood had to be functional as well as attractive; after numerous designs were tested, they chose one for the SRT and a different one for the GTS. A Ram-like honeycomb grille had to be dropped, because it interfered with airflow in extreme conditions.

The underhood area was carefully styled, and most viewers were drawn to the huge X-brace which dramatically increased torsional stiffness.

Buyers wanted an interior that matched the nearly-six-figure price tag of the car, and now they got one; it helped that Sergio Marchionne had pushed for investing dramatically in interiors to counter years of Daimler cost-cutting. The idea was to match cars costing two or three times in interior quality and performance alike. For Viper, the benchmark was Porsche – not Cadillac or Corvette.

Klaus Busse had been lauded for his work on the

Ram pickups; now he worked his magic on the Viper as well. Busse opened up the work to any designer, even if they were already on another project; many worked on sketches in their own time, for review by Busse and Gilles. Tome Jovanoski's evolutionary design made the cut; he led the final development of the horizontal theme, influenced by the original 1996 GTS. The hood's 'power dome' influenced the vertical center stack.

Gilles wanted to wrap as much of the interior in leather as possible, including the instrument panel and door panels; parts were created with the wrapping in mind, avoiding problems later. The idea came from European specialty cars, where leather-wrapping was standard; while labor-intensive, it cut tooling costs. The Viper ended up having smaller and more consistent gaps between panels, thanks to advance planning and computer modeling.

The two models, SRT and GTS, required different approaches. The GTS was leather with Alcantara inserts, in black, black with red, and black with caramel (a rich light brown); buyers could also opt for Laguna leather in black or sepia (tan). SRT buyers would get a high-quality cloth, integrated with vinyl, and chosen because its extra friction would help in hard cornering. Leather was optional for the SRT.

Team Viper held a competition between seat options at a major Viper owners' meet. The winning entry was a Sabelt thin-shell racing seat with the ability to take a six-point racing harness and a 1.6in (4.1cm) height adjustment.

The seat was lower and further back, for larger customers; the console dropped by the same amount to match it.

The team had a full size clay model in late October of 2010, which they scanned to create initial CAD files. 'Easter eggs' went into the design, a trend that had started at Jeep; for the Viper, they included a snakeskin motif on the rear turn signals and the snake-eye look of the headlights.

Graham Henckel's engineers were cutting weight in the meantime; like Dick Winkles, they went for gains wherever they could find them. They put ideas onto a big board and organized them by cost, benefit, and feasibility. Since the retail price wasn't fixed, they were able to use expensive materials including carbon fiber (hood, roof, decklid), super-form aluminum (doors), and the existing cast magnesium dash structure. The Track Pack was even lighter than the stock car, thanks to lighter wheels and rotors, coming in at 3297lb (1495kg).

CAN bus had come and gone with Daimler; Chrysler was working on a new system called PowerNet, using 6 million lines of computer code and a mile of wire which was actually a saving from the CAN bus. As others developed parts, surfaces, and colors, the integration engineers, electronic engineers, and coders worked the bugs out of PowerNet.

Henckel rented a group of supercars for benchmarking, including two different Ferraris, a Jaguar, Lamborghini, Mercedes SLR, Bentley, and a Corvette ZR-1. They concluded that the supercars, particularly the SLR, didn't

GTS-R special edition, taken 2016. (Author)

live up to magazines' praise; and that the Viper still had an advantage over many of them. Dodge's tremendous torque was still unique, and the car had more of a raw feel – true to its origins. The team felt it could beat most of its more expensive competitors in fit and finish, as well, but now it had something concrete to measure against.

The 2013 Viper had new rear suspension geometry, a new interior, and a slightly wider front track; the brakes were the same size, but buyers could opt for a cast iron rotor and aluminum hub which, with lightweight wheels, cut around 50lb (23kg). The team had lost many of the original suppliers, so using existing parts didn't always reduce tooling costs, freeing it to change what it wanted to; Ralph Gilles claimed, perhaps in jest, that the only carryover part was the windshield. The old plastics were sacrificed for more-controllable carbon fiber and aluminum.

Just before the Viper was launched, Chrysler decided to make SRT its own brand, separate from Dodge; so there was no 2013 Dodge Viper after all. It was an SRT Viper or an SRT Viper GTS.

ONE CLUB BECOMES TWO CLUBS
In 2010, DaimlerChrysler sold a large supply of Viper parts and materials (including wheels, transmissions, parts made in discontinued colors, body panels from the Viper Competition Coupe, and parts and tooling from the first generation cars) to the Viper Club of America (VCA). The car was no longer in production, and nobody wanted DaimlerChrysler to scrap the parts; but DaimlerChrysler could not sell them directly, either.

The Club agreed to donate some items to museums or private collections, keep some for their historical value, distribute some to regional clubs, and resell some to generate operating funds. It created a for-profit company (Viper Parts of America) and paid the Club president, Christopher Marshall, and a friend to run it. It also paid Chris to publish *Viper Magazine* and to manage the Invitationals; his wife was the club's paid Executive Director. As time went on, there were accusations of sweetheart deals, lack of return to the Club, and suspending competitors from Club membership or sponsorship; in response, Club members and officers were dismissed.

In 2013, the irreverent auto site *Jalopnik* published a leaked letter from Chrysler to the VCA president; the company was concerned that the club and business activities were not separated enough. They needed a wall between the for-profit side and the nonprofit side; the same people could not run both.

Viper enthusiasts, disenchanted with the VCA's leadership (and in some cases ejected from the VCA), created the Viper Owners' Association (VOA). The VCA's own founding president, Maurice Liang, became the founding president of the VOA, and continues to publish the club magazine, *Viper Quarterly*.

In time, the management of the original Viper Club of America changed; Viper Parts of America was dissolved and its assets were sold to Jon Brobst and partner Don Scharf Automotive, who formed the new 'Viper PartsRack of America.'

In 2019, the Viper Owners Association (driveviper.com) boasted over 1700 members and published an award-winning magazine; it had 36 active regions around the world, and hosted bi-annual National Viper Events. At the first two National Viper Events, the VOA gave away a new Viper as the door prize – an incredible giveaway.

The Viper Club of America (viperclub.org) is still around, and is open to non-owners as well as owners; in 2019, it had roughly 500 paid members. Most of the regions are no longer around, and the magazine is no longer published, but they still hold invitationals every other year.

IN PRODUCTION
The new car was first shown to dealers on September 14, 2010, with an expected sale date of 2012. Painted 'Candy Apple Red,' the fifth generation Viper (body code VX) was, in Sergio Marchionne's words, "something magic, unique." It recalled the original Viper's lines and curves, but was still new.

The car was revealed to Viper owners at their national convention, less than a month later; there was no advance hint of what was coming, but then, in smaller groups, owners were led into a special room. After seeing various other new products, they were shown the model on a turntable. Some owners loved it; some thought it had been tamed too much (which was, in fairness, a criticism of the 2003 as well). Production had already been authorized.

Fittingly, the first public unveiling was led by Ralph Gilles at the New York Auto Show. The list price was $99,390 for the SRT (including destination), and $122,390 for the GTS; the gas-guzzler tax pushed the price for the base model into six figures even on the SRT. With inflation, prices were not all that much higher than on the 2010 models, though the six-figure total had a psychological impact. Delivery charges were probably break-even or lower than the real cost, since the cars were sent to dealers by covered truck.

A wider range of colors was available than on the original Viper; the Candy Apple Red paint used on the model was included. Likewise, two types of stripes were now included, full-length stripes that went from the front aero pieces to the tail (optional on the GTS) and shorter ones that just went from hood to deck lid (optional on SRT).

There were still changes in store for the 2013 Viper before it hit production; aero and track testing had revealed issues that had to be resolved. Hundreds of hours of wind tunnel time were used to cut drag while maintaining downforce. The car was put onto a 'shaker machine' which could simulate many miles of driving on poor surfaces without damage to a human driver. The shaker could find problems with the frame design, the actual construction, the materials, and such – anything from the doors falling off or frame cracking, to squeaks and rattles in the dashboard. Every car Chrysler produced spent some time on the shaker.

How was the Viper received, you may ask? Original Team Viper leader Roy Sjoberg said the upgrades were good. Jon Brobst, the pace car driver for the SRT Viper Cup since 2010 and owner of PartsRack.com, test drove a loaded 2013 Viper GTS on the track. The experienced six-foot-three Viper driver reported that comfort and ergonomics were both better than the 2006 First Edition, and he liked the new power seat up/down, fore/aft, and recline features, along with the usual adjustable pedals; he particularly praised the chubby/flat-bottom steering wheel. While many Viper owners traditionally prefer 'back-to-basics,' Brobst appreciated the reconfigurable controls and the large displays, along with the grained leather 'everywhere.' But all this, one could find out from a stationary car.

After taking the car around the track, Brobst reported that "even from the paddock ride, this Viper felt better." The steering was responsive from low speeds onwards; at high speed, the car "feels glued down flat on the (dry) track." He liked the street settings for pace laps, and on the rough surface of the paddock, they were relatively comfortable but still responsive. After a while, driving guests around the track, he switched to track mode, and stayed there, saying that on hot laps, "I began to fine-tune my appreciation for how amazing this fifth generation Viper really is; total control, not scary, geared just right. Planted. Responsive handling, noticeably improved. The extra 40 horsepower feels like even more, due to the 3.55 rear differential and reworked transmission ratios."

After a while, it started to rain, and he reported, "I had no reason to worry! Just drive the heck out of it, wet, and it turns, brakes, and accelerates with confidence-inspiring responsiveness. No drama, just hooked-up control."

Enthusiast Scott Thomas bid $300,000 to buy the first Viper at a charity auction; on January 10, 2013, he took delivery from Sergio Marchionne, CEO of Chrysler, and Ralph Gilles, head of SRT. The Conner Avenue plant now had around 150 employees building roughly 12 cars per day; production had begun on December 5, 2012, but Thomas' car was the first to be completed.

The 2013 SRT Viper had polished 'Rattler' wheels, four-wheel Brembo brakes, stability control, HID headlamps,

Contrasting the Viper with a Challenger Hellcat. (Courtesy Marc Rozman)

and LED running lights and tail-lamps. Inside, buyers got the 7in customizable gauge display, 8.4in center screen, backup camera, navigation, Performance Pages, Launch Control, 12-speaker stereo, and adjustable pedals. The new color palette included red, silver metallic, gray, yellow, blue, black, and white.

A 2013 Viper GTS Launch Edition, inspired by the 1996 and 2006 special-edition coupes, was done up in GTS Blue with dual, full-length white stripes.

The 2013 SRT Viper was actually cheaper than the Chevy competition, the Corvette ZR1 ($113,000). The GTS, on the other hand, would set a buyer back around $125,000; but that was cheaper than a Porsche 911 Turbo ($138,000) or Audi R8 V10 ($153,000). Even so, Chrysler reported just 591 US Viper sales for calendar-year 2013 – and seven in Canada. (They also sold 20 in calendar-year 2012).

After the 2014 model-year started, SRT said they had built 805 Vipers for the 2013 model year, but had only sold 426 of them; so they cut production by a third, going from nine cars per day to six. At that time, only 443 dealers in the United States were allowed to sell the cars, partly because they had to pay $25,000 and take special training

courses to be authorized by SRT; and, for obvious reasons, dealers tended to be reluctant to provide test drives. The company addressed both issues.

The new Vipers certainly had better comfort and performance, and were more than competitive with pricier cars; but the high price was a stumbling block for a Dodge-labelled car, and inventories started to grow.

For 2014, SRT showed off a new Viper model, the Viper TA – unlike the old T/A (Trans Am) muscle cars, TA allegedly stood for 'Time Attack.' The two-mode Bilstein Damptronic suspension was tuned for the track, with firmer damping and a smaller spread between modes than the GTS; dampers, springs, and stabilizer bars were all retuned, and the aluminum X-brace over the engine was replaced with a lighter carbon fiber version. The brakes had two-piece, 32mm wide rotors and pads with high thermal capacity, and the carbon fiber front splitters and rear spoiler boosted downforce by a factor of seven. Curb weight was 3390lb (1538kg).

The company planned to make 93 cars in a special TA Orange, 33 in black, and 33 in white; an earlier announcement had planned just 33 cars, all orange, but demand for the special edition was higher than expected. The package was

more than just looks; a Viper TA set the Laguna Seca track record.

In January 2014, SRT showed off a new Stryker Green color, based on 2008's Snakeskin Green but with enhanced pigments and a 'liquid mercury' look; it took around eight hours to paint each Viper with the new color.

SRT also launched a new Grand Touring package between the base SRT and the luxurious GTS; the Viper GT added $10,000 to the SRT price, and provided Nappa leather seats with Alcantara inserts, a two-mode sport suspension, five-mode stability control, the GTS hood, two-piece StopTech slotted rotors, red Brembo brake calipers, and a power six-way driver seat.

The final racing Viper was unveiled in late 2013. Designed for the United Sportscar Racing season, Sports Car Club of America, North American Road Racing Association, Pirelli World Challenge GT Class, and International GT3 Championships, the new car was dubbed GT3-R; the first car, purchased by Ben Keating and raced as part of the Riley Motorsports team, was given the number 33, and first ran in the 24 Hours of Daytona.

A 50-car run of Anodized Carbon Special Editions in 2014 had metallic matte paint that "adds depth while the dark matte color amplifies the Viper's sinister quality," according to a press release. The car was sold in standard and TA form, and had black-chrome Rattler wheels, gloss black badges, satin black exhaust bezel, orange calipers, and carbon fiber brake ducts and rear appliqué; the interior had Alcantara and Nappa trim, with orange accents.

Buyers could also get a Time Attack Group for the GTS, which added the rear spoiler, front corner splitters, two-mode Bilstein dampers, P Zero Corsa tires, solid sway bars, and fade-resistant brakes; that provided the comfy GTS with the Viper TA Special Edition performance parts.

On May 6, 2014, Chrysler announced that it was dropping the SRT brand. There was also some controversy as Chrysler destroyed 93 pre-production Vipers from 1992; these were built without full emissions or safety gear, and were not legal for driving on public roads. Chrysler used them for development, then donated them to schools. Two of the cars were crashed on public roads, and Chrysler brought them back to destroy them so they couldn't be driven illegally. Legally, Chrysler was probably unable to do anything else, but some fans were distressed to see the carnage.

SRT tried to balance things out; they had increased the 2014 Viper's price by $2000 over the 2013, to $104,480 including destination, but they also threw in the Grand Touring Package (GT) and 12-speaker stereo, which had been $4495 in 2013. The 2014 Viper came with a 900-watt amplifier, navigation system, and three-mode stability control (a rain mode was added to the former street and track settings). The GTS was upgraded with two-piece

StopTech rotors from the Track Package and a five-mode stability control including the rain mode. Sidewinder II wheels and Pirelli Corsa track tires were moved from the track package to become freestanding options; and the Viper TA switched from StopTech rotors to two-piece Brembos. Finally, SRT Viper buyers could get their cars painted Billet Silver and GTS-R Blue, to echo the #91 GTS-R American Le Mans racing car.

After that didn't move the sales bar, Dodge gave $15,000 coupons to current Viper owners to encourage them to buy a 2014, and then took $15,000 off the list price of the 2015 Vipers. By October 2014, the head of Dodge said he had 200 orders for 2015 Vipers in hand.

Where did the $15,000 discount come from? Some claimed that was the cost of running the factory racing program, which stopped at the end of the 2014 season

– a season SRT and Dodge had won. Cutting the price boosted US Viper sales by 29% over the prior year, hitting 760 – still low by historical standards. This was a shame, given the new Viper's strengths.

The base 2015 Dodge Viper SRT cost $87,490 (including destination), in the same territory as prior generations despite the pricier materials; the GT added, for $10,000, Nappa leather with Alcantara inserts, a two-mode sport

Snakeskin. (Original from Roy Sjoberg and Warren Steele)

The final Dodge Viper with the last Dodge Challenger Demon – the latter including an 840hp (626kW) supercharged 'Hemi Hellcat' V8 engine. Dodge auctioned off its new and old image leaders, donating the proceeds to charity. (Courtesy Gene Yetter)

suspension, five-mode stability control, GTS hood, two-piece StopTech slotted rotors, red Brembo brake calipers, and a power six-way driver seat.

There was a new model in early 2015: the GTC, where they promised to only make one car with the exact same options and colors, for a base price of $94,995 plus destination. The GTC provided a personal concierge, let buyers follow the build process on-line, take a personal tour of the factory, and choose from 8000 paint options, 24,000 stripe colors, ten wheel options, 16 interior trims, and six aerodynamics packages. Dodge threw in a Viper speed-form replica to confirm the colors, and a personalized instrument-panel badge. Only retail buyers could get a GTC; dealers couldn't order one for the showroom. It was a true bargain for a car of the Viper's caliber.

Midyear, the company returned to making the GTS ($110,490) and a TA 2.0 Special Edition. The latter was $6000 more than the Viper GT, but added a rear spoiler and front lower dive planes, two-piece Brembo rotors and performance pads, Matte Black Sidewinder wheels, Pirelli P Zero Corsa Tires, a dual-mode suspension, five-mode stability control, black brakes with orange lettering, carbon-fiber X-brace over the engine bay, rear carbon fiber appliqué, front splitter and aero wing assembly kit, TA markings, and a car cover.

The GTS added Laguna leather-covered seats, Alcantara headliner, and Nappa-covered trim; an 18-speaker sound system; polished aluminum Venom wheels; and power six-way driver and passenger seats. The GTS Ceramic Blue Special Edition had black stripes, orange calipers, and rear carbon fiber appliqué. The various special editions didn't perform any miracles, and US Viper sales sank to 676 for calendar-year 2015 (with 14 sales in Canada, and some sales outside Dodge's two primary sales outlets).

While the US list price for a new 2015 Viper might have still seemed excessive to some Americans, it could be far worse; in China, they were paying over $480,000, between the unfavorable exchange rate, gray-market margins, and import tariffs. Dodge itself did not import the Vipers; at least

one Chinese importer (Beijing Tuning Street) bought them and shipped them over.

RETURN OF THE ACR

The new Dodge Viper ACR was unveiled in May 2015, and was sold in the 2016 and 2017 model years; the starting price was $117,895 plus destination and gas-guzzler taxes.

Designed for racing, the car had track-tuned aerodynamics; with the optional Extreme Aero Package, it boasted 2000lb (907kg) of downforce at 177mph (285km/h), roughly double the prior ACR. That came from a rear diffuser, carbon-fiber front air treatments, hood with removable louvers, front splitter with a detachable extension, more dive planes, and a six-foot dual-plane adjustable rear wing. The rear diffuser ran all the way up to the front axle, with six removable strakes that rubbed against the track surface to improve stability and high speeds. The suspension had coilover Bilstein racing dampers with three inches of height adjustment and ten settings for rebound and compression (adjusted by a pair of clearly marked knobs at the top of the coils); the springs had 600lb/in (107kg/cm) and 1300lb/in (232kg/cm) ratings, more than double the Viper's usual numbers.

As a result of the upgraded suspension, aerodynamics, and tires, the Viper ACR could maintain 1.5 g in turns. The top speed was limited to 177mph (285km/h), though, sacrificed for better downforce.

The ACR also had new carbon ceramic brakes with six-piston calipers, supplied by Brembo, the Viper's traditional brake-maker. The front rotors were 15.4in (39.1cm), with the usual six-piston calipers, and the rears were 14.2in (36.1cm), with four-piston calipers. Front brake ducts helped keep things cool.

The tires, created for the car, were Kumho Ecsta V720s, at 295/25R19 front, 355/30R19 rear – almost absurdly thin sidewalls; the tires alone apparently had a huge effect. The electronic stability control was also retuned, with five modes provided for extra control; the engine and transmission were both stock.

Team Viper used a lightweight carpet, three-speaker audio, manual seats, and lightweight brakes, to hit a weight distribution of 50/50. Buyers had grippy Alcantara leather inside, with accent stitching. Those wanting a unique car could pony up for the GTC 'one of one' customization option, guaranteeing that nobody else could get their combination of colors and options.

The Viper team's focus on cooling and running full-out for hours without losing performance worked; in *Car & Driver*'s 2016 Lightning Lap trials, the Dodge Viper ACR beat every other car in the competition, which included a Ferrari 488GTB, Porsche 911 GT3 RS, Corvette Grand Sport, McLaren 570S, Acura NSX, and Acura R8 V10 Plus. The Viper's track time of 2:44.2 was almost a full second better than the second-place Ferrari, and nearly three seconds ahead of the Porsche. The Dodge Charger SRT Hellcat finished 13th, with a time of 3:03.5, the fastest four-door car present.

Perhaps more relevant, by November 1, 2015, the Viper had set records at 13 different tracks: Laguna Seca, Road Atlanta, Waterford Hills, Nelson Ledges, Motown Mile, GingerMan (extended length), Pittsburgh (north track), Grattan, Virginia International (grand course), Willow Springs (Big Willow), MotorSport Ranch, Buttonwillow, and Inde Motorsports Ranch (configuration four).

VIPER VARIANTS

Prefix, which worked on the Viper engine and painted its body panels, introduced a 'Medusa' convertible conversion for the 2013-17 Viper series, at $35,000 (the company only made ten of them). Owners could also get a Targa roof, like a T-top, but without a bar running down through the opening; owners could remove the center section of the roof, while keeping the back glass. This cost $10,000, and included a carbon fiber roof panel that could be removed and stowed in the trunk.

The VLF Force 1, first shown in 2016, used the Viper chassis and drivetrain with carbon-fiber panels and new styling; they retuned the engine and had different suspension calibrations. Buyers had a choice between the manual transmission and an automatic; just 50 were planned, with prices starting at $268,500.

SPECIAL EDITIONS AND THE END

The end of the Dodge Viper was officially announced in June 2016; there were a few reasons for shutting down the line, including increased safety requirements. Not only did the Viper have no room for side airbags, as one example, but they may have been incompatible with the electronics architecture. Sales had fallen, and Dodge now had its Hellcat Challengers to lead the way and grab magazine covers and Web headlines. It was time for either a new Viper, or an end to the program...and they had not developed a new Viper.

Dodge announced that they would make 206 Vipers in five special editions, with numbered plates and personalized covers, to celebrate the car's 25 years. All had Kumho Ecsta V72 tires and black-and-red Alcantara leather – well, all but Snakeskin and dealer specials.

The Viper 1:28 ACR (28 cars) celebrated the car's 2015 track record at the Laguna Seca Raceway, with its 1:28.65 lap time; it was blue with red ACR stripes, including the Extreme Aero package, carbon ceramic brakes, an exterior sill decal, ACR interior, red accent stitching, and car cover matching the paint scheme. Buyers had to pay $138,795 total for this car; the package itself was $11,000. (The carbon fiber pack cost $5,100; the ACR added $19,000; and the Extreme Aero cost $6,900. The ACR interior was another $6,000).

Likewise, the GTS-R was celebrated by the Viper GTS-R Commemorative Edition ACR (100 cars) – faster to drive around the track than to write on the page – painted white with a blue stripe, to recognise the racing cars. Reflecting the 1998 GTS-R GT2 Championship Edition, this car had the Extreme Aero, carbon ceramic brakes, and red badge decal and seatbelts. The 100 to be made reflected the 100 Championship Editions celebrating the Viper's win of the 1997 FIA GT2 championship. The price of this car ended up at $140,245 – including $350 for the red seatbelts.

To celebrate the GT2 further, Dodge bought a hundred disposable cameras, with 36 frames of film in each one; the cameras were numbered 001 to 100, just like the GT2 cars, and were used as 'assembly cams.' As the camera rode down the assembly line on the car, workers at each assembly station took a photo or two of the process. Buyers got the camera along with a letter from plant manager John Hinckley, advising owners that six photos were left for them to record the delivery and first drive; the letter urged owners to process the film carefully, saving the camera body as a souvenir, in an auto-industry 'factory first.' (Jon Brobst wrote that the photos were mainly of smiling Viper builders with thumbs up and the car at each station.)

The Snakeskin GTC (25 cars, all , with a custom snakeskin-patterned SRT stripe) reflected the 2010 Snakeskin ACR; it had the advanced aero package, GT black interior, and custom car cover, and used Pirelli P-Zero tires rather than the Kumhos of other special editions. Likewise, the interior had black suede and leather seats, rather than the Alcantara coverings of the other specials. The total, $113,795, was far lower than the others, as a result.

Finally, there were the VoooDoo II ACR (31 cars, black, with a graphic metallic ACR driver's stripe bearing red tracer outlines, at $136,095 including various required options); and dealer editions for Tomball Dodge and Roanoke Dodge (22 cars, total), part of a program that was open to any dealership. The dealer edition ACR was white with a Competition Blue center stripe, Adrenaline Red driver stripe, carbon ceramic brakes, Extreme Aero package, and ACR interior.

In case you wondered, yes, the name was definitely 'Vooodoo II,' with no fewer than five 'o's.

The 1:28 Edition sold out in 40 minutes; the VoooDoo II took two hours, the other two corporate editions lasted

ACR 1:28. (Author)

around two days, and the two dealers sold out their own customized specials in five days. For that reason, Dodge added a special run of 31 Snakeskin ACR cars. This had the exterior paint and stripes from the Snakeskin ACR, coupled with an ACR interior, the Extreme Aero Package, carbon ceramic brakes, a personalized car cover, and a dash plaque.

Viper ordering and production stopped in October 2016; many expected that to be the end, but, in December, Dodge reported that it had only stopped because it ran out of headlights and ACR body parts. It reopened the order banks in December 2016, without any more special edition plans, but buyers could only order cars that the company had the parts to make. It was an odd way to wrap up the series, but an eminently rational (or cost-effective) one.

Overall, Dodge sold 630 Vipers in the United States during calendar-year 2016, and, despite or because of the end-of-the-line announcement, another 585 during 2017. Another 19 stragglers left dealerships during 2018.

The final Dodge Viper was auctioned off in June 2018, along with the very last Dodge Challenger SRT Demon, with the proceeds going to the United Way. The Viper Red 2017 car (and the 2018 Demon, hand-painted the same shade of red) sold for exactly $1 million, and auctioneer Barrett-Jackson added a 10 per cent buyer's premium which was donated to the American Heart Association.

Those who wanted a piece of Viper history could bid on 1800 bits of it: when production ended, Dodge put related memorabilia up for sale, including eight signed hoods, hundreds of prints, merchandise, and a Viper GTS sketch signed by Bob Lutz, Tom Gale, and François Castaing. The auction, whose proceeds went to the United Way, ran from March 12 to April 13, 2018. A great deal of Viper history – including the cars – was scattered throughout the world, fitting for a car that demanded, and got, respect from people who may never even have heard of Dodge before.

TEAM VIPER SURVIVES

The tight-knit team that created the Viper still meets from time to time, sometimes at Roy Sjoberg's place, sometimes on request for public appearances. It says a great deal about the cohesiveness of the team, forged in the heat of creation, that they still get together, over a quarter century after the Viper stunned the world. (Photo courtesy Roy Sjoberg and Warren Steele)

8
Factories

The first Vipers were made at a prototype-building facility on Mack Avenue, on the east side of Detroit. Roy Sjoberg said the Motor City location of the plant was no accident; they wanted to build the car within the Detroit city limits.

The Mack Avenue plant started out as a Briggs Body factory in 1916; Chrysler bought it with 11 others in 1953, and finally closed it in 1979. While it was closed, thieves broke in, stealing transformers to get the oil inside and spilling contaminated oil on the way out. The City of Detroit bought the site in 1982, hoping to resell it, but couldn't find a buyer; finally, in 1990, the city, the EPA, and Chrysler worked together to clean up the asbestos and PCBs. They had to remove 11 million gallons (42 million liters) of contaminated water from the stamping pits and power-wash 18 acres of walls and floors to clean the site.

The Mack Avenue plant sat next to the new Jefferson Avenue plant which pumped out Grand Cherokees; it occupied the site of old Chrysler offices and showrooms. A small airport was close by, while many of the side streets brought views of hundreds of small houses on streets bereft of curbs, on roads that continued going straight as far as the eye could see. It was an odd place to visit, with almost completely silent land on the other side of the main roads; while, behind extensive landscaping, factories silently (from the outside) churned out Jeep Grand Cherokees, Dodge Durangos, and V6 engines.

When Roy Sjoberg first visited the facility, he said, "We thought the plant was deserted; we unlocked the door, walked in, and saw a huge concrete building inside the plant. The architect from plant engineering was with me, and he said, 'There's no cinderblock building in here.' So we went over and knocked on the door, and there were about 15 guys having coffee."

They weren't vagrants; they were Chrysler employees, skilled workers who had been dedicated to the facility – and forgotten. They were inside the plant, but they thought it was too big, and it wasn't air-conditioned. The masons, electricians, and plumbers in the group had built an air-conditioned cinderblock building within the plant.

Roy continued, "Inside the plant were desks and all kinds of facilities, and they brought them all inside the cinderblock building; and that became our headquarters. With those 15 guys who weren't on Chrysler's head count, we built the first conveyor line and all the facilities we needed. We had the 15 guys who provided us the skilled trades."

Once the Viper was in production, Lee Iacocca came for a tour (and to get the first car, since it was earmarked for him). He was surprised at how compact the assembly area was, with only 26 stations to build the vehicle. Frames were delivered already assembled, and body panels were created and painted at the ASC plant, but that wasn't unusual; even steel body panels are usually done at separate stamping plants.

Around 200 people worked in groups of five, with no moving assembly line; when they found problems, they could open up a discussion with Team Viper to find solutions. The finished cars' dimensions were verified by computer-controlled laser-wielding measuring machines. Whether anyone at Chrysler was aware of Pehr Gyllenhammar's work at Volvo in the 1960s (recounted in *People at Work*), the system was somewhat similar: small teams worked on a large number of tasks, with a conveyor system that moved and then stopped until the work was done. New Mack had used teams of five; the later Conner Avenue plant generally used two people per station, working for 45 minutes (versus around 45 seconds at a typical plant). The lower volume meant many changes in how parts were staged, not to mention a great deal more training for each plant worker.

Despite starting late in the year and using a craftsman-team approach, they were able to build 310 cars in 1992 (some of them were 1993 models). The peak capacity was cited as being around 5000 cars per year.

Some onlookers expressed doubt that they could ever sell thousands of cars, much less thousands per year; *Road & Track*'s Ron Sessions pointed out that Shelby had built only 400 Cobra 427s, and the mighty Honda was having a hard time selling 3000 Acura NSX sports cars in the United States. As Sessions pointed out, what were the prospects for a roadster with no automatic transmission or air-conditioning?

Team Viper took the unusual move of making the factory pleasant for visitors. Chrysler (and, later, DaimlerChrysler and Fiat Chrysler) generally did not encourage members of the public to visit their factories; even reporters were only invited in on special occasions. But with New Mack and then Conner Avenue, buyers could come and visit the plant, albeit usually as part of a club tour. Roy Sjoberg told a group that they tried to make "a facility that people would enjoy going to; in fact, while we were in production, I think we made more money on the knick-knack store than we made on the car, because everybody came out – and typically they'd spend a couple of hundred dollars."

As time went on, Chrysler needed the Mack facility to make a new series of engines, and the Viper team was sent to find a new place. (The complex was later merged into a single giant Jeep/Ram assembly plant.) Team Viper found its new location on the far side of the Jefferson Avenue plant, on Conner Avenue; it was surprisingly close.

The Mack plant had been cleaned up before Roy Sjoberg arrived; the Conner Avenue plant had not, and making it clean was not easy. Created by Champion to make sparkplugs, the building had been shut down after 20 years, then used for storage. Still, it was in the right location, and it was the right size.

Chrysler bought the Conner Avenue building in mid-June, and hired a number of contractors on a 24/7 basis to clear and clean the plant, upgrade the facilities, and prepare for the arrival of the tooling. Hauling the materials that had been stored in the plant took a long time in itself; and once it was emptied out, it became clear that it would take an enormous amount of work to clean out all the talcum powder that had been used for making porcelain sparkplug insulators. Anyone who has spilled talcum powder at home can see that having the stuff float through the air for two decades would cause quite a mess, especially in such a large space.

Despite the challenges, the new home of the Viper was producing cars in late September, a fast changeover by

Building a 2013 Viper. (Courtesy Jerry S Mendoza)

anyone's standards. Every Viper from the 1996 RT/10 was made at Conner Avenue.

In the late 1990s, the plant made roughly eight cars per day, with nearly four days between the day work started on a car and the day it ran down the final inspection line. Along the way, it went through 31 stations.

The car started with a Fabco frame which arrived with the cowl assembly attached; the team separated the cowl assembly, adding everything from pedals to the air-conditioner, while another group put the brake lines, fuel lines, and wiring onto the frame. Then they attached the differential, the suspension, the brakes, and the now-complete cowl assembly. Then came the engine and transmission, followed by under-hood support systems and the fuel tank, the exhaust system, and the aluminum transmission tunnel plate. This was roughly the same way it had been built back at Mack.

At this point, the car was aligned with camber, caster, and toe in front and back, using a machine created for the Viper which could set front and rear camber to 0.002°. They also took an almost-unique step: making sure that, when the car hit a bump, the toe angle did not change. That required measuring the change in the toe angle and both ends of a simulated bump; the computer then told workers which shim to put between the steering gear and frame, to avoid bump steer entirely. Aligning a Viper at a local shop could take up to three hours, given the exacting measurements and need for four-wheel alignments.

From there it was easy: drop the car to the floor, fill all the fluids (by machine), and start it up. Then it was 12 minutes in the test booth, running over rollers at 90mph (145km/h) and making sure everything worked well; then the brakes, suspension, and such were checked. This was all done before the body panels were put on, partly because problems would be easier to spot, and partly because it was easier to fix anything that went wrong. That's one advantage of a panels-on-spaceframe design – it would be next to impossible on a unibody.

The body was put on starting with a fiberglass assembly at the rear of the car, both bolted and glued to the frame, to hold other panels. The interior was set up next, before the roof (on coupes), which made it easier to install the seats, console, and trim. The next steps were adding the various body panels: the roof, rear quarter panels, taillight panel, and such, followed by the headliner, windshield, doors, hood, fender liners, fascias, headlights, and inner door trim panels. The Viper then had its headlights aimed and went through a long, careful detail.

People from other plants who wanted to work at Conner took tests and were interviewed at the plant, then put into line for the next opening. There was more to the job than craftsmanship. In the early 1990s, Chrysler had started to ask its employees how to make the processes more efficient, raise quality, and cut costs; in some plants, millions of dollars per year were saved by acting on these ideas.

Makers of the first 2013 SRT Viper. (Courtesy Jerry S Mendoza)

One change, detailed by Daniel F Carney in *Dodge Viper*, regarded the cowl assembly; they started out by carrying an entire cowl assembly from the frame, adding the instrument panel, steering wheel, electronics, and, starting in 1994, air-conditioning; then they returned it to the frame, which required lifting and moving it numerous times. Plant engineers gathered together a group of employees for several days, and they created a carousel which rotated the assembly from one station to the other instead of moving it through four stations. They also had better access to the parts they were working on.

Low-volume cars tend to have a large number of fit and finish issues. The factory addressed this by using laser-festooned computer rigs which measured the frame and attachments precisely, to show exactly where to put body panels and such, and, if needed, where to add which shims to line the panels up. It was a good solution; before Mercedes launched its S-based limited-edition luxury car, the Maybach (whose volumes turned out to be lower than expected), it sent a team to Conner Avenue to see how it was done on the Viper.

A 2001 press release declared that every Viper was built by workers with over 300 hours of car-specific training; the car itself included over 50 component modules. Stamping, welding, instrument panels, casting, and painting were all done elsewhere (the composite body panels were pre-painted, which required a surprising amount of care in shipping). According to Chrysler, "The Conner Avenue Assembly Plant operates more like a race shop than a conventional automated assembly line." At each work station, people were their own inspectors. They still tested bump steer, and set the alignment with the wheels in three different positions; and they still roll-tested at up to 90mph.

In late 2002, Conner Avenue started building engines as well, making it (at the time) the only assembly plant to also build its engines. (The block was cast elsewhere, but it was machined at Conner).

The 2003 Viper was changed somewhat to ease production, part of a trend that started at Chrysler with the original Viper and LH cars. Targets for precision in body and interior panels had increased over the past ten years, and gaps or misalignments that had once been acceptable were no longer good enough.

When Viper production ended in 2010, the plant was abandoned; nobody knew that a new Viper was on the way, and so the clean, carefully renovated facility wasn't secured or preserved, even after work on a new Viper was started later the same year. That was a problem for the team that had to ready the plant for the 2013 series; and so, once again, Team Viper had to empty and refit Conner Avenue, repainting, replacing light fixtures, refreshing the concrete floors, and replacing production equipment. It also installed a "metrology center" – essentially, Chrysler's old computer-guided measurement system, but updated to current technology.

As with Chrysler's 1990s CATIA-based 'virtual factories,' engineers created a virtual assembly line in the computer, to make sure every operation was possible and to get the timing just right, so nobody would be scrambling to keep up and nobody would be waiting for something to do.

The new setup included more robots, for greater precision and speed; they could make holes exactly the right size, rather than having them larger than necessary so bolts could be moved to line things up. It was still quite a human-dependent process; with the old crew retired or dispersed, around 150 new people had to be recruited from other plants, tested, and brought in.

The Viper V10 was still built on-site, each engine dyno-tested for 40 minutes before installation. The engine took around nine hours to build, even with pre-assembled heads.

The 2013 Vipers were made at the rate of one every 32 minutes (12 per day), built roughly the same way: moved on a line, one step at a time, sitting at each station for 32 minutes and then moving. Dodge claimed in 2015 that it took between 140 to 160 hours to hand-paint each car.

The last Dodge Viper was made in August 2017; bright red, like the first, it was to be auctioned with the final 2018 Dodge Challenger Demon.

Could they have sold more? Tim Kuniskis, Global Head of Alfa Romeo and Head of Passenger Cars – Dodge, SRT, Chrysler and FIAT, FCA – North America, addressed that question:

"In the last year of Viper production, we introduced the record-setting Dodge Viper ACR, which set 13 lap records at race tracks across the country. We developed five serialized special editions models for 2017 to commemorate the 25th Anniversary and end of Viper production, and we introduced the Viper One-of-One program, which allowed customers to … choose from 50 million unique build configurations, made up from the more than 16,000 unique paint (gloss or matte) color options and more than 48,000 unique stripe combinations.

"Could we have sold more? It's a great question. We are in business to sell cars, so it's always a good thing when we sell more. But we are also in the business of building a brand and engaging our customers, and with the last-generation Viper, we can say that the majority of the last Vipers built are custom, one-of-kind race cars that will never be duplicated; and that, too, is something valuable to our performance enthusiasts who own these cars, and who also have Dodge Charger and Challenger Hellcats and Jeep SUVs and Ram trucks in their garages and driveways."

Finally, in March 2018, Fiat Chrysler announced that the Conner Avenue plant would be cleaned out once again, and converted to an internal space for meetings, storage, and showing off 85 of Chrysler's historic cars and trucks. The original Walter P Chrysler Museum, first opened in 1999, had closed in 2016 to provide Alfa Romeo and Maserati with office space; now there would be a new spot for company personnel to see and be inspired by Chrysler's historic cars.

9
Racing

The first Vipers to enter Le Mans were run by the Rent-a-Car Racing Team, which converted roadsters by adding hard tops. Drivers Justin Bell, René Arnoux, and Bertrand Balas finished a respectable third in the GT1 class, tenth overall. Bell later pointed out that the aerodynamics were less than ideal, with the front lifting at 190mph.

The GTS coupe and its race-ready version, the GTS-R, were engineered side-by-side; Roy Sjoberg claimed that, since Viper production was already sold out, the sole reason for racing was to improve the engineering. Whether Lutz and Iacocca agreed that racing would be worth the expense as just a development cost, or whether they felt Chrysler needed European exposure and credibility as the company was trying to re-establish itself as a global concern, doesn't really matter.

By now, using the methods which had brought the Viper out in under three years, Chrysler was pumping out one hit car after another. The LH cars, best known for the Dodge Intrepid, revolutionized large cars and revived a dying segment. The next hit, the Neon (sold under the Chrysler, Dodge, and Plymouth names) easily outperformed every other car in its class in acceleration and cornering when launched, which led to a long dominance of its class in SCCA racing. It even made a profit, which no other American compact had done for a while.

Chrysler, stocked with world-class cars again, was reaching out for sales in long-abandoned regions. Gaining notoriety as winner of European-dominated motorsports was one way to show off its new cars to European buyers.

To reinforce what Roy Sjoberg said, though, if the company only wanted an image and racing presence, it could have had a custom car built with Viper styling, NASCAR-style. Instead, its race-ready Viper was closely based on the 'civilian' model. Indeed, Roy Sjoberg later said, "Everybody wanted to change it and we said, 'No, no, you've got to run it the way it is. The only way we'll learn what breaks and what doesn't break is if we race it as a production engine.'"

Racing provides faster feedback than engineers would normally get; endurance racing quickly exposes a car's strengths and weaknesses. Chrysler's engineers had their own test regimens, some of which were very

The winning Dodge Viper GTS-R with the track dirt intact. (Courtesy Patrick Rall)

tough indeed (especially the off-road tests for Jeeps), but professional racers could push cars harder, in different ways, than the standardized tests. The pros also had the ability to articulate some issues that only came up on the track, so having engineers working directly with racing teams helped both sides.

The faster pace of development could be habit-forming, or so Chrysler's leaders hoped; once incubated in the forge of Team Viper, young engineers could be sent around the company, infecting (so to speak) other groups with their sense of urgency and working directly with end-users. At least one member of the racing team agreed that Chrysler meant this to be a learning experience, to help people think under pressure, and come up with good, innovative solutions under pressure.

The development engineer for the GTS-R was Neil Hanneman, who had four SCCA championships under his belt and had been hired away from Shelby Enterprises. McLaren helped with aerodynamics, partly because it had a moving-ground wind tunnel, the most realistic way to simulate high-speed driving. The primary beneficiaries of that work were the GTS-R rear spoiler and ground effects.

The GTS-R was officially unveiled in 1995, at the Laguna Seca track in Monterey, California. The company had two teams, one which was based in nearby Canada (Canaska/Southwind). Each team got three GTS-Rs and a set of engineers, who mainly focused on the engine, while the teams dealt with tuning the chassis.

After around one year, Team Viper started working with a single team from François Castaing's rolodex. Racing driver Hugues de Chaunac had created ORECA

in 1972; the name is short for Organization Exploitation Compétition Automobile. Hugues de Chaunac reportedly pushed the pace of development, his personal credibility helping Team Viper to win arguments with any corporate brass who were used to a less demanding pace.

The first season was spent in the GT1 class, but other automakers had started running racing cars with little relation to their production versions, so they decided to move to the GT2 class, which enforced more commonality between 'cars you can buy' and 'cars you race.' GT2 cars have relatively few modifications for racing, making them closer to stock.

The two teams seemed to have a great deal of respect for each other; the Chrysler people, particularly those on Team Viper, held Team ORECA in high regard, and the name 'ORECA' appeared frequently in press releases. Likewise, the ORECA people had high praise for the Chrysler people, acknowledging that some of them were new to racing – but that they were willing to learn.

Dodge and ORECA's efforts paid off almost immediately; in 1997, a Viper GTS-R won the FIA GT2 class world championship – the first time an American automaker had even won the world championship with a production-based car. It was not bad for an automaker which hadn't been at Le Mans for 65 years. The 1997 wins were no fluke; the Viper won the FIA GT2 championship again in 1998, and then, after FIA reclassified its competitions, won the GT class in 1999. Entering (and winning) just five out of eight races in 1999, Vipers took the Drivers' and Manufacturers' American Le Mans championships.

Above and below: Inside the winning GTS-Rs. (Author)

Vipers won't only winning at Le Mans: Bobby Archer drove a Viper to win the SCCA GT championship in 1999, as well.

By this time, Vipers were competing against (and beating) the Corvette C5-R; and Team ORECA was coming up against other GTS-Rs entered by independents. These ranged from 34th to 93rd place in a field of 119 cars, beating a host of pricier cars.

Vipers won the entire race, not just its own class, at the 2000 Rolex 24 at Daytona. Once again, this was the first time an American car, based on a standard-production model, had ever won. It was a surprise victory; originally, Team ORECA wasn't even going to take their Dodges to Daytona. Lou Patane, head of motorsports, made the call to race in November 1999, only around eight weeks before the race. The winning car was driven by Olivier Beretta, Karl Wendlinger, and Dominique Dupuy; three Vipers and two Corvettes would each take the lead at one point or another.

The team followed that up with first, second, and third places at the 12 Hours of Sebring, and the LM GTS team championship in the American Le Mans series.

For years afterwards, the winning #91 car was given a place of honor at the Walter P Chrysler Museum, along with its trophy; the museum left the car in its immediate post-race condition, covered in dirt and mud, with all the nicks and scratches preserved. One of the docents, Pete Hagenbuch (former head of Chrysler production-engine tuning), said it was hard to keep the cleaning people from washing the dirt off the car, and claimed that it was, as time went on, getting cleaner, rather than dirtier.

This was the last year for the Team ORECA/Team Viper partnership, but in just a few short years, the Viper GTS-R had gone from birth to dominating tracks normally considered the property of high-end Italian and German companies. Winning 42 world-class competitions from 1995 to 2002 drowned out the idea that the Viper was just an American muscle car incapable of going around corners; it was a true sports car, a step above the Corvette and a direct challenge to Ferrari, Porsche, and other factory teams.

In 1998, the Viper GTS-R finished first and second in its class (GT2) at the endurance-focused 24 Hours of Le Mans – and in 1999, Vipers finished first through sixth in their LM GTS class, with the company cars accompanied by four private teams. In 2000, Vipers took first and second place in the GTS class at Le Mans (seventh and ninth overall), with a third car coming in fifth in class (12th overall); another Viper GTS-R, run by independent Carsport Holland, came in sixth (13th overall).

Dodge Vipers weren't even sold by Chrysler dealers in Europe when the team started racing the car – though some gray-market cars were brought in before the "Chrysler Viper" was officially launched. New chapters of the Viper Club of America were formed across Europe in the wake of the GTS-R's racing success.

There were actually three racing engines available on the GTS-R; the standard motor was the usual 8L V10, with 525hp (391kW). The 750hp (559kW) engine rested at the top end, and a 650hp (485kW) option was in between. All were for racing only; none could be registered for street driving. To get that extra power, Team Viper changed the aluminum block casting to insert a thicker iron sleeve in the cylinders; the entire cooling jacket was changed to keep a desirable compression ratio. A lightweight flywheel spun in a magnesium bellhousing, to keep weight down and make the engine a little more responsive.

The chassis and suspension were tuned differently for the track alone than they were for both street and track, and the extra power demanded a good deal of change to other systems regardless. Meritor (née Rockwell) supplied GTS-R springs, and Koni provided the shock absorbers (dampers). Body panels were carbon fiber and Kevlar, to reduce weight.

Drivers had to learn to use the shifter gently, albeit quickly, to avoid breaking transmission parts. The transmission was strengthened over time, but drivers also learned to work with it well enough to keep it going through 24-hour endurance races. Racers got essentially the same transmission as regular buyers, with upgrades to deal with the added torque; and the changes made for racing filtered to the production cars.

The racing Vipers were surprisingly good in wet weather, due partly to tire choice and the weight balance. The engine was smooth, too, which helped; and, despite early problems with the shifter, as well as its long throw, at least one driver praised it. The steering was actually taken from the production car, though with solid, rather than rubber, bushings.

The biggest problem to sort out might have been heat, with the massive engine and side exhaust taking up much of the interior space. The teams tried heat resistant coatings and special paints, to no avail; they started developing air-conditioning, but didn't install it.

Vipers were quite cheap for successful racing cars; they cost around $325,000 each. Yet, they captured GTS class and drivers championships in American Le Mans (ALMS) for 1999, and the class, manufacturers', and drivers' championship in 2000, after which they retired from the series.

One can ask why Chrysler left racing. One answer is that they needed more resources for creating a new Viper. It's more likely the reason is that Chrysler was acquired by Daimler-Benz, whose leaders were developing a new Viper; another was that the company had been acquired by Daimler-Benz in 1998, and the leaders in Stuttgart were less enthusiastic about the benefits of the Viper racing program than those in Michigan had been (it didn't help that the Viper would theoretically compete with the Mercedes SLR).

Regardless, the Viper had already left its mark with its sudden, dramatic success; it also cleared the way for the Corvette team. It was not the end of the Viper on European tracks, though; it was more of a hiatus.

Viper GTS-Rs were still run on European courses after 2000. Team ORECA and others fielded GTS-Rs in the 2001 Le Mans, but did not do quite as well. Independent teams also competed with GTS-Rs in the 2002 Le Mans; the top Viper finished in 14th place overall (third in class), beaten by two factory-team Corvette C5-Rs. Three of four GTS-Rs in this year's Le Mans finished, all in the top 25 (out of 56). Two Viper GTS-Rs were in the 2003 Le Mans; one came in 16th overall (fourth in the GTS class). It would be the last year of the Viper GTS-R at Le Mans.

Dodge returned to racing Vipers with the 2004 Competition Coupe, a non-street-legal car eligible to compete in the Grand Am Rolex Series and SCCA Speed World Challenge; it had a slight power boost to 520hp (387kW) and 540lb-ft (732Nm), coupled with a carbon/Kevlar body to cut weight.

Tommy Archer drove a Viper Competition Coupe to the 2004 SCCA GT championship, after working with Dodge's PVO (Performance Vehicle Operations) team on developing the car. He had won the Trans Am Series Rookie of the Year Award earlier, in a Dodge Daytona, and had made Dodge's first Trans-Am win in 25 years at the Detroit Grand Prix. In 1997, driving with Justin Bell, Archer had five podium finishes with the GTS-R, driving his Viper to class seconds in both the 1998 24 Hours of Le Mans and the 1999 24 Hours of Le Mans. In 2000, he dropped down to fifth place at Le Mans, still a respectable finish.

In 2007, Dodge won two championships on two continents: a Viper Competition Coupe won the new FIA GT3 Championship in Brazil, beating cars from Ferrari, Lamborghini, and Porsche, among others. Team RPM won the British GT Championship in a Viper, finishing with 81 points; that was six points ahead of their closest competitor, Barwell Motorsport, which was running V12-powered Aston Martins. In that year, Dodge had sold 25 Competition Coupes, a sales record for that car; from 2003 to 2007 combined, Dodge had built 120 of them.

THE VIPER RETURNS

The first 'post-shutdown' racing configuration was the 2014 Viper TA (Time Attack), a street-legal car which could run at over 150 road-race courses around North America. This car is described in some detail in Chapter 7. But for American Le Mans' GT class, something else was needed – the result was the GT3-R.

This car, selling at an estimated $460,000, had an efficient aero package, Xtrac six-speed sequential transmission with paddle shifters, a multi-disc racing clutch, and lightweight wheels. As Ralph Gilles said, though, "Like every Viper race car, the GT3-R is a direct descendant of the SRT Viper street car." Dodge, focusing on American tracks, hired Riley Motorsports to carry the flag.

The GT3-R ran in the GT Le Mans class of the first International Motor Sports Association (IMSA) TUDOR United Sports car Championship series. Their first win was at 'the brickyard,' the Indy 500, narrowly beating a Ferrari

458 Italia, Porsche 911 RSR, and Chevrolet Corvette C7.R. The other SRT Viper came in at #8, slowed after a collision with a Mazda prototype.

At the final race, on October 4 at the Petit Le Mans, the two-car SRT team won the series' team and driver titles for their class, and two of three class championships; they finished second in the GTLM manufacturer championship.

The Viper was again invited to join in the 24 Hours of Le Mans, but did not fare as well as in past years. Just two Viper GTS-Rs ran, coming in 24th and 31st overall, out of 56 entries. Within their LMGTE Pro class, the results were two Porsche 911 RSRs, an Aston Martin Vantage GTE, a Corvette C6.R (from GM's factory team), two Ferraris, another Corvette, and then the Vipers, followed by a Ferrari and two Aston Martins. It could have been worse: numerous cars failed to finish, laid low by mechanical problems, and the Viper had been hobbled by an engine restrictor, not to mention flat tires.

After winning an American Le Mans championship in endurance racing in 2014, Dodge dropped their factory Viper-racing program. The production car had not been selling well, and the program allegedly added $15,000 to the cost of every Viper. By dropping the racing program, Dodge could cut the price of the 2015 Viper by $15,000, which increased sales more than racing success had.

Riley kept going without Dodge's sponsorship, with Jerome Bleekemolen and former Viper Cup champion Ben Keating driving the #33 GT3-R, now sponsored by Viper Exchange. Ben Keating had already piloted the #33 car to a triumph at the 2014 Grassroots Motorsports Ultimate Track Car Challenge, beating, among other cars, an Audi R8 Turbo, Corvette Z06, Nissan GT-R, Dodge SRT4, 1970 Camaro, 1968 Mustang, and Porsche GT3R. Keating's track time would have won the pole position at the American Le Mans Series race at the same track in the prior year.

Their independent Riley team stayed in the middle of the pack for a while. The Dodge Viper ACR-X brought Lee Saunders a win in the TA3 class in the first event of Trans Am's 50th season, in 2016; he was ninth overall at the Sebring event. The #93 Dodge Viper GT3-R finished third in the GT Daytona class at the 2016 24 Hours at Daytona, and 16th overall; the #33 car finished tenth in class, and 24th overall.

In October 2016, Ben Keating, Jeroen Bleekemolen, and Mark Miller captured the Petit Le Mans' checkered flag in the Riley GT3-R #33 at Road Atlanta's 2.54-mile track. It was the final run for the Viper in IMSA/WeatherTech Sports car Championship competition. Keating said, "The goal was to give it a good send-off. Viper has such a rich racing history, and to do our last race in the Viper with IMSA at Petit Le Mans and go out on top is a huge deal."

Bleekemolen won the pole position and ended up coming in second after a rules infraction sent an Audi to the back of the pack. With additional wins at Belle Isle and Road America, the team ended up in second place (in points) for the 2016 season, beaten only by a Ferrari 488 GT.

Another winning Viper: car #53, as it ran at Le Mans. (Courtesy Patrick Rall)

The 2016 Dodge Viper ACR holds 13 records at tracks including Laguna Seca, Road Atlanta, and Virginia International Raceway. The Sports Car Club of America (SCCA) certified that the 2016 Viper ACR held more track records than any other production car in the world – not a bad way to end a production run. Eleven of those records were set by Chris Winkler, one of SRT's vehicle dynamics and development engineers. Professional racer Randy Probst set the record at Laguna Seca, 5.27 seconds faster than the prior ACR's record there and 1.24 seconds faster than his own record in the $845,000 Porsche 918 Spyder.

THREE LAPS OF AMERICA
The One Lap of America series had drivers traveling around 5000 miles, then competing at 12 different racing venues with their street tires. A wide variety of cars, both independent and factory-sponsored, new and classic, entered the event; they ranged from low-end mildly modified classics to high-end sports cars, but all had to be street-legal. A 2000 Dodge Viper GTS won the championship in 2000 – and in 2001 – and in 2002.

OFF-ROAD RACING
In 2011, Mopar (Chrysler's aftermarket branch) unveiled its new, 800hp (597kW) V10 Competition Race Engine. Within weeks, a Ram 1500 powered by the engine made its debut

in the Tecate SCORE Baja 1000 – and helping Kent Kroeker and Alan Roach to win their class (Class 8). They had to cover nearly 700mi (1127km) of rugged terrain in just over 20 hours to win.

LAND SPEED RECORD
In the late 1990s, lead development engineer Herb Helbig led a team seeking a land speed record. They took out all the unnecessary weight they could from a stock 1998 GTS, added a roll cage and other safety gear, and put in a GTS-R engine. Its speed in the A/GT standing mile (nearly 194mph, or 312km/h) set a record which lasted for years afterwards.

In 2007, Karl Jacobs drove an E85-powered Viper at Wurtsmith Airport to 220.7mph (355km/h), a new record for the standing mile in a street car, but he was assisted by a twin-turbo package, magnesium wheels, new suspension, and numerous other parts.

DRAG RACING
On October 1, 2010, Dodge unveiled a V10 powered Challenger designed solely for drag racing. The Challenger had a Viper V10 engine with a two-speed automatic transmission and ran in the Stock Eliminator and Super Stock configurations; it was the first drag-race package car in history to have an engine over 500 cubic inches.

Herb Helbig's 'Blue Lightning,' a 1998 GTS with some equipment removed and safety gear added, which set a land speed record of 193.97mph (312.2km/h) in the A/GT class. (Original picture courtesy Patrick Rall)

The package used competition wheels and tires, a solid rear axle, integrated roll control, a fuel cell, and race-ready interior. The list price was $85,512, with a $7950 package adding an eight-point roll cage, six-point harness, and mesh window net; and any color besides white would cost $6800. Buyers had to apply to buy the car, which was definitely not street-legal.

Shortly after the launch, Dave Thomas set an NHRA national record in the Sportsman class, piloting a V10 Drag Pak; Jeff Teuton won the US Nationals the following year with a similar car, in the Stock Eliminator class. Overall, Mopar Dodge Challenger Drag Packs (as the company called them) with the V10 engine claimed many NHRA national and divisional class wins, and continued to compete long after production stopped.

AT THE 'RING (AND SOME OTHER TRACKS)

Dodge took the Viper down to the Nürburgring track in Germany, one of the most demanding tracks in the world, in August 2008. The engineers had no experience at the track, and had just one day to prepare and one to drive, in poor weather.

Tom Coronel, who had driven a Viper at Le Mans, set a record in his third lap, beating the old 7:34 time. That would have been enough for some people; but he kept driving, and in his fifth lap, he broke his own new record, hitting 7:22.1, a time that would stand for three years (it was finally broken by GM, running a 2012 Corvette C6 ZR1, in June 2011). He was only able to drive six laps, but it was enough – and it also led to some changes. Based on his experience, the engineers modified the 2010 Viper ACR to have a shorter fifth gear ratio, to get higher speeds down the front straightaway of Döttinger Höhe and past the Antonius Bridge. The rear wing profile and end plates were retuned to improve yaw downforce for greater speeds through high speed turns, and a shorter-throw shifter allowed quicker shifts.

Did Dodge's changes make a difference? A scant six months after GM broke Coronel's production-car record, Dominik Farnbacher recaptured it, running a 2010 Viper ACR at Nürburgring. The run was sponsored by SRT and the Viper Club of America, and used two Viper Exchange cars, on September 14, 2011. Farnbacher's best time was 7:12.13, seven seconds faster than the Corvette and ten faster than the 2008 Viper. That time also bested the Porsche 911 GT3, Porsche 918 Spyder, and Lexus LF-A Nürburgring Package. (This story is told in far more detail in Maurice Liang's *Return* book.)

Viper concept car with the #91 GTS-R in 2017. (Courtesy Marc Rozman)

The Viper ACR set records at other tracks, as well. In late 2009, Viper engineer Chris Winkler took a 2010 Viper ACR around the Laguna Seca course in under 1:34; while it was an unofficial run, it broke the old record, set by the Devon Motorworks GTX prototype (Devon was owned by Justin Bell, and the GTX was closely based on the Viper). The prior track record, 1:35.117 seconds, had been set by another Viper in 2009. Likewise, in April 2010, Kuno Wittmer ran a 1:59.995 lap at Miller Motorsports Park, making the Viper ACR the first production car ever to beat two minutes on the 3-mile outer course.

Years later, Dominik Farnbacher returned to the 'Ring to drive a 2017 Viper GTS ACR to an unofficial run time of 7:03.45, easily beating the Mercedes AMG GT R's 7:10.92; no officials for record-keeping agencies were on hand, but witnesses vouched for the time. Mechanical issues and rain prevented a second try. His effort was crowdfunded, to the tune of $164,900, along with Viper Exchange sponsorship. The time was fine, but people wanted more – an official run and a better time.

In one final effort in 2017, a crowdfunded group set a track time of 7 minutes, 1.3 seconds (7:01.3) on the Nürburgring track, using a completely stock 2017 Dodge Viper on stock tires. That was a superb time for a relatively affordable, high-production car (by 'Ring record standards), especially one run by privateers. It gets more impressive: driver Lance Arnold made the new time on his first lap. After that, a 160mph (257km/h) tire failure resulted in collisions with both guard rails, also setting off the airbag. Lance said he could have beaten 6:57 (the time set by the all-wheel-drive Porsche 918 Spyder) with a little more time on the track.

Many Nürburgring records are set by well-resourced manufacturers' teams, who use multiple cars over multiple days, seeking the ideal weather. The Viper team had five hours – and still beat all other rear-wheel drive stock cars.

*Dodge's One Lap of America winner.
(Original picture courtesy Patrick Rall)*

A journalist checking out a 2013 GTS-R at its New York unveiling. (Courtesy Jeremy White)

The final Viper GTS-R series. (Author)

10

Truck and motorcycle

A few specialty companies used Vipers and Viper engines for their exotic cars, but Chrysler was the only one to put its motor into a motorcycle and pickup truck.

DODGE TOMAHAWK

The Dodge Tomahawk concept motorcycle had four wheels to handle the 2003 engine's insane 525lb-ft (712Nm) of torque and 500hp (327kW) of horsepower. The engine was cooled by twin aluminum radiators, mounted atop the intake manifolds; the Tomahawk took nearly as much coolant (11qt, or 10.4L) as gasoline (13qt, or 12.3L).

The exhaust used equal-length stainless-steel headers with dual collectors and central rear outlets. The electrical system was quite beefy, with a 136 amp alternator and 600 amp battery; the headlights, barely perceptible when shut off, consisted of 12 5W LEDs with masked lenses; the taillamp used eight LEDs.

There was no doubt that this was a powerful machine when it started up; clouds of blue smoke betrayed low-friction rings, the huge throttle bodies were clearly visible up front (where a headlight would normally be fitted), and the throaty rumble made it clear that a thrill ride was in order. The motorcycle had a good deep note, but wasn't necessarily louder than other motorcycles; it was simply devoid of any shrillness or high notes. Dodge listed 0-60mph (97km/h) times of just 2.5 seconds, with a theoretical near-400mph (644km/h) top speed.

Power went to the wheels via a two-speed foot-shifted transmission, a sequential racing-style setup with a dog ring and straight-cut gears. The first gear ratio was 18:38 and the second was 23.25. A double-disk dry clutch was activated by hand lever, with an assist. Dual 110-link chains were needed to carry the power.

The four wheels each had their own independent suspension, and parallel wheels were separated by a few inches. The front suspension used single-sided parallel upper and lower control arms, made of billet aluminum and mounted via ball joints to steering uprights and hubs; it was set up with 5° of caster. There was a single adjustable coilover damper, using a 2.25in (5.7cm) coil.

The rear suspension used box-section steel inboard swing arms and included an hydraulic parking stand. The

Tomahawk motorcycle. (Author)

damper was a single adjustable Koni coilover design, with the same size coil as up front; it had a pushrod and rocker-actuated linkage. Steering was a dual-hub setup.

Front and rear, the racing-style hubs were a center-lock design. The brakes had massive 20in (51cm) drilled rotors, one per wheel, with machined stainless steel in front and cast iron in back. There were two four-piston front calipers per wheel; in back, a single four-piston caliper made do for each wheel. Custom-designed calipers were anodized blue; drivers activated front brakes by hand, and rear brakes by foot controls.

The driver sat just 29in (74cm) off the ground. The whole thing was estimated as weighing 1500lb (680kg).

Pushed through by chief operating officer Wolfgang Bernhard, the Tomahawk was earmarked for production at $200,000 each. The actual build price was over $100,000, but the engineering costs had to be amortized as well. The plan may not have been as well thought-out as one would think; US law proclaims a motorcycle can only have, at most, three wheels on the ground during normal operation. The Tomahawk would have been classified as a car, which would subject it to safety or lighting requirements it couldn't pass. That said, it might have passed muster in other regions.

Chrysler built ten more Tomahawks, and sold them through luxury retailer Neiman Marcus for $555,000 each – as 'rolling sculptures.' Buyers could drive them, but not on public roads, and presumably not with any sort of insurance. Chrysler kept the original for its museum.

The Tomahawk may actually have paid for itself, both through the Neiman Marcus sale and the publicity. The Viper-powered motorcycle made a huge splash, and helped to keep Dodge's muscle aura alive – likely selling a good number of the new Magnum V8 wagons.

DODGE RAM SRT-10

Would you believe a 2004 pickup that could do 0-60mph (97km/h) in 5.2 seconds, with a 13.8 second quarter mile and 0.92G skidpad? Some in 2004 couldn't, but there it was.

Dodge had been selling Ram 2500 and Ram 3500 pickups with truck V10s for some time when the Ram SRT-10 appeared; the heavy-duty iron-block ten-cylinders weren't speed kings, but they were good torquers. The Dodge Ram SRT-10, in contrast, was meant for fun, not towing. The truck was a good idea for Dodge's image; people who shrugged at Magnum SRTs and Vipers were intrigued by it. Those lucky enough to drive one had to constantly stop, lift their hoods for curious pedestrians, and rev the engine for truck guys.

The first showing of the production truck took place in February 2003. The deep front fascia, front splitter, and rear wing had all been tuned from time in the wind tunnel; as with the Viper, the goal was to balance drag against downforce. A new 'power bulge' hood was needed for the extra-sized engine, because the SRT-10 was based on the Ram 1500, not the 2500 (there was no iron-block V10 version of the Ram 1500).

Inside, designers did what they could with the workaday interior, adding black-on-white gauges, bolstered leather seats with perforated black suede inserts, and carbon fiber trim. The Viper's red start button went onto the dashboard; a custom Hurst shifter with a Viper-type shift knob went

'Viper-powered' Ram SRT-10. (Author)

into the center console, and aluminum pedals with rubber grips dressed things up a bit. Drivers got the usual panoply of six gauges, which stayed in trucks long after they left cars, with a big tachometer (including nearly 2,000 rpm of "useless zone" above redline) and a 160mph (marked to 240km/h) speedometer.

The seats were good for gripping the driver in hard turns, and the standard features – dual-zone a/c, power six-way driver's seat, 508-watt, eight-speaker stereo, wheel-mounted audio controls, overhead console, and heated foldaway mirrors – kept the driver comfortable on long trips. However, drivers had the inconvenience of getting out to fill the tank more often than in a standard Ram; the SRT-10 pickup was rated at just 9mpg (4km/L) city, 12mpg (5km/L) highway – making the Viper look like an economy car.

The sole transmission was the Viper's manual six-speed; the differential was the Viper's version of a Dana 80, with a 4.11 ratio (changed to 4.56 after the first year). The truck did need a new cooling system, based on Ram's heavy-duty setup, along with a custom dual exhaust and manifolds, a new oil pan, and transmission mounts. Much of the front suspension and steering was taken from the Ram 2500, with new struts, rear sway bar, and Bilstein shocks; the massive wheels were shod in P305/40R22 Pirelli Scorpion tires (front and rear wheels were both 10in wide). Antilock brakes were standard, with new 15in (38cm) rotors for the front brakes and existing Ram 2500 rears. As with the Viper, the front fascia included brake cooling ducts.

Designers gave the Ram a special front and rear fascia and grille, a rear spoiler, and a large chrome Ram badge; the suspension was lowered by 1in (25mm) to help with cornering.

In February 2004, Brendan Gaughan, who had won six races for Ram in the NASCAR truck series, took a stock Ram SRT-10 to a two-lap, both-directions run of 154.6mph (248.8km/h) at Chrysler's proving grounds, in an event certified by Guinness and the SCCA; that was 7mph (11km/h) over the past record.

For 2005, Dodge changed the axle ratio from 4.11 to 4.56 and added a 'quad cab' (four-door) with two rows of seats and an automatic transmission. The 48RE automatic was borrowed from the high-torque Cummins diesel option, but it still needed a heavier duty torque converter and two-piece driveshaft. Owners could tow 7500lb (3402kg) with their high-performance rig. The original regular-cab, manual-transmission version was still available; the quad cab was sold only with the automatic, the regular cab only with the manual. For both trucks, SRT used new four-piston calipers and a standard body-color tonneau cover.

The Viper engine was smooth and controlled in the truck, feeling like an ordinary V8 while the throttle was at reasonable levels; the automatic transmission tuning helped, reacting normally until heavy throttle. Then the transmission would make a sudden hard shift and the truck would leap away.

It was two trucks in one; you could drive it to work, tow a trailer, or take your gran to church, shul, mosque, or Ethical Culture Society. Later, you could take it out to the track or set a new speed record for going to work. The normal engine note was a good deep growl; under full throttle, it was a racing car. A quick blip at idle took the engine right to high revs; on the freeway, a few short seconds of thrilling acceleration took the truck into illegal territory. The engine was instantly responsive, regardless of where it was on the tach before, and the transmission could kickdown instantly when needed.

Cornering was good for a big pickup, but that's a huge caveat. Nobody would take a Ram 1500 SRT-10 out to a road course and try to beat Corvettes or even Camaros. It dealt well with tough spots like sudden acceleration in the middle of a turn; part of its secret was the anti-spin differential, which helped to keep the tail from swinging out too badly under provocation. Like the Magnum and Charger SRT cars, any loss of traction was quickly resolved by letting off the throttle. The ride was firm, but there was little jouncing and bouncing, and it wasn't so stiff as to be bone-rattling; rough streets weren't a punishment.

Acceleration was quite good for the era, with a 0-60mph (97km/h) time of 5.2 seconds and a 0-80mph (129km) in 8.4 seconds; it could do the quarter-mile in 13.8sec at 106mph (171km/h) and had a rated top speed of 150mph (241km/h). The truck weighed 5100lb (2313kg) with a regular cab and 5450lb (2472kg) with a quad cab, and the ground clearance on the quad cab was a hefty 16.5in (41.9cm), more than triple that of the Viper.

The price of the 2005 Dodge Ram 1500 SRT-10 was $57,460, not including various options like red paint ($225) or side airbags ($490). Dodge did not release production figures but the Viper Truck Registry, which warns that the numbers are probably inaccurate, estimated around 3057 were sold in the United States in 2004; 4127 in 2005; and 1973 in 2006, its final year, for a total of 8837. It's possible that more than 10,000 trucks were made, since they were also sold in Canada for 2004-05, but these totals weren't included in the list. The one year for which it does have separate figures for Canada and the US, 1653 were sold in the States, and 320 in Canada (a disproportionate number went north of the border that year).

Sales figures may have given some ammunition to those wanting an automatic-transmission Viper: the Quad Cab outsold the Regular Cab 2465 to 1662 in the first year both were sold, and 1301 to 672 in the second year. The lesson is ambiguous, though, given that 3057 Regular Cabs (manual transmission) were sold in the first year, and that you could only get four seats with the automatic.

SRT-10 engine under the Ram hood. (Author)

11

Chrysler flagships and Dodge derivatives

DODGE'S DERIVATIVES

The Viper was an awesome boost for Dodge's image; could the company capitalize on that in the mass market? Tom Gale seemed to believe the Viper's success opened the door for more specialty cars; but under the penny-pinching leadership of Bob Eaton, the door stayed firmly closed. Three cars show how Dodge might have followed through on the Viper.

The 1994 Dodge Venom concept, a lightweight car using the Neon floorpan with a 245hp (183kW) V6 and rear-wheel drive, got midrange buyers' hopes up, but it never reached the assembly line. The car would likely have been quite a hit, bolstering Dodge's street credibility at relatively little cost, and fans continued to wish for it for years afterwards.

For 1997, another Dodge V10 concept was shown: the Sidewinder, a retro-rod using parts of the Dakota pickup. The car had 488 (8.0L) graphics, a four-speed automatic, and a removable roadster soft top. To start it, the driver flipped a switch labeled 'arm,' starting the fuel pump, then pushed a button marked 'ignite.' The goal of this car would likely be to amortize the continuing costs of Viper development by spreading the investment to a second car with many shared parts … or it might just have been a show attention-getter.

The production-intent 1997 Dodge Copperhead prototype was to sell for $30,000. The rear-wheel drive car focused on superb handling, with wheels at the extreme ends of the body, and power coming from a 2.7L V6 connected to a five-speed manual. The chassis was closely based on the Viper itself; it was popular at the car shows and in Internet forums. Like the Sidewinder, this car could have amortized the investment in the Viper frame, chassis, and special parts, lowering the company's costs for either car; and it might have done quite well in parts of the world where fuel costs made Vipers less attractive.

Renamed 'Dodge Concept Vehicle' after a name conflict, the Copperhead was killed by DaimlerChrysler. Outside of select journalists and employees, only *Gran Turismo* and *Gran Turismo 2* gamers could drive it.

Chrysler 300, with Maurice Liang. (Courtesy Maurice Liang)

CHRYSLER FLAGSHIPS

Tom Gale believed that every brand should have its own flagship, to tell customers and the company itself what it was all about. The Viper created an image of Dodge that the company had to work up to. After the Viper, Plymouth got the Prowler; that led to the PT Cruiser and, if Gale had his way (he did not), new versions of the company's minivan, midsize car, and large car. That would have readied Plymouth for the crossover craze, while pushing Dodge, Chrysler, and Plymouth further apart in appearance and utility. In retrospect, Gale's plan would probably have been more successful than killing Plymouth entirely and assigning its cars to Chrysler, which is what DaimlerChrysler actually did..

The search for the Chrysler flagship was never completed. The first major concept was arguably the 1991 Chrysler 300, which used the Viper V10 and an automatic transmission; the car was 28in (71cm) longer and 7in (18cm) taller than the Viper, perhaps to fit the automatic transmission.

The 1991 300's interior had a sporty feel, with a driver's pod that was fully separated from the passenger seat; the driver's pod was done in black, and the rest of the interior in tan. Instead of a key, there was a slot for magnetic cards; inserting one would position the seats and mirrors for the owner of that card, while opening a door covering the ignition switch. There were also rear seats; Maurice Liang quipped, "The one 'spinoff' I wish they had pursued was the '91 Chrysler 300 concept car that used the Viper engine and chassis. Then you could take three friends for a ride instead of one at a time!"

The 300 concept had a plush, comfortable interior, with suicide doors that gave access to a tight rear seat area. It was created as a production-intent vehicle, with steel body panels and street-legal lighting, capable of meeting US safety standards of the time – which suggests that it was seriously considered as an automatic-transmission version of the Viper, to get customers who didn't want to go all the way back to basics. The frame was also based on that of the Viper, and the iron-block V10 in the concept came from an early Viper mule; but there was much more sound insulation than in the Viper.

Roy Sjoberg summed up the 1991 Chrysler 300 as "a stretched Viper and fully drivable. I was sorry it didn't fly; a four-door would have beaten the market."

The 1995 Chrysler Atlantic was supposedly based on the experience of Tom Gale and Bob Lutz as judges of the Pebble Beach Concours d'Elegance. Designed by Bob Hubbach and influenced by French coupes of the 1930s, the Atlantic was powered by a 4L straight-eight, made from a pair of Neon engines put together nose-to-tail.

Next up was the Chrysler Phaeton, a dual-cowl luxury

Above and left: Chrysler Chronos. (Author)

concept with retro-modern styling and an outrageous V12 engine to go past the Viper's V10 (or maybe replace it in a future model). The 48-valve, 5.4L V12 engine was probably created from Chrysler's new 2.7L V6 engines, merged either by hand or by CATIA. The intake manifold vaguely resembled that of the company's 3.5L V6, which was in the same family. It's possible that the Phaeton was only done to get publicity for Chrysler, with absolutely no real production intent; but it might have been testing the waters for a fully modern V12 for future Vipers.

The stunning Chrysler Chronos lent its front end look to the later 300C; this car had some Viper lines, and, like early versions of that car, no outside door handles

(replaced by a button on the key fob). The interior resembled a fine classic English car, modernized. The engine was a V10, but not the Viper version; it was a 6L overhead cam design, and built from Chrysler 4.7L V8s. The suspension was largely taken from the Viper.

Had this car been built, it would most likely have used the already-engineered Viper V10, with a similar spaceframe body; but it would have been tuned for more comfort and easier driving, with a heavier weight, and (as the concept had) an automatic transmission. Then again, given François Castaing's desire for modern engine technology, the Chronos' V10 and the Phaeton's V12 might both have been design studies to replace the Viper's relatively dated setup. Castaing was pushing for the Viper to break new ground with its next generation, and one can't imagine he was happy with the two-valve-per-cylinder wedge engine.

After Daimler took over, Chrysler did an ME 4-12 prototype car with a top speed of 240mph (386km/h) and a quarter-mile time of 10.6sec. The transmission was a Ricardo and Chrysler-developed double-clutch setup with automatic shifts and steering-paddle overrides. It took a mere 6.2sec to reach 100mph (161km/h).

There were two secrets to the ME 4-12's performance; one was lowering weight to 2880lb (1310kg) by using more lightweight materials and a unibody structure; the

Above: Sidewinder. (Courtesy Marc Rozman)

Right: Chrysler Firepower concept at the Chrysler museum. (Author)

other was a V12 engine provided by AMG which pushed out a stunning 850hp (634kW) and 850lb-ft (1150Nm). Wolfgang Bernhard, Chrysler's chief operating officer, told the world that the ME 4-12 was "a prototype that will be road-ready by summer." Alas, the Chrysler would have been cheaper and faster than the Mercedes SLR; and the ME 4-12 was parked in the basement of the Walter P Chrysler Museum rather than produced for general sale.

The 2005 Chrysler Firepower was closer to the Viper, and essentially what many had been calling for since 1992. It used the Viper frame, suspension, and brakes with an SRT V8 engine and automatic transmission. The Firepower would have finally provided a cheaper, more

comfortable car, easier for normal people to drive, but still boasting sporty looks and high track performance. Given body code ZD (which shows someone was serious), the Firepower had a steel body and was positioned against the Corvette, with a proposed price of around $60,000.

Rumors of a Chrysler version of the Viper continued until the day the Viper was officially cancelled. The

Chrysler ME-412. (Author)

rumors kept going because they made sense; a Chrysler Firepower would have amortized the Viper's tooling and design costs across a higher volume, and opened sales up to those who wanted more luxury or an automatic transmission. The case against was whether it would sell against the Corvette and upscale German and Japanese coupes, and, while DaimlerChrysler existed, whether it would hurt Mercedes' sales or reputation.

While it lasted, the Dodge Viper was, in Herb Helbig's words (quoted by *Automobile* magazine), "the singular,

most purpose-built American sports car. Its performance was the best value on the planet."

The Viper stayed at the top for a much longer time than anyone thought it would; even when the "Hellcat" Hemi V8 raised the Challenger and Charger to a new level, they could not outrun the Viper on a road course. The Viper was a fine match of American muscle and European handling, combining bountiful torque with superb cornering. Through Chrysler's entire history, from 1904 to the present day, no car was quite like it.

" ... the singular, most purpose-built American sports car. Its performance was the best value on the planet ... "

Herb Helbig

12
Selected Viper specifications

Sample specifications were chosen from years after the initial launch of each generation, because early spec sheets could be prone to error.

ROADSTERS AND CONVERTIBLES
Lengths reported in inches (mm)

	1993	1999	2005	2009
Wheelbase	96.2 (2444)	96.2 (2444)	98.8 (2510)	98.8 (2510)
Track (F/R)	59.6/60.6 (1514/1538)	59.6/60.6 (1514/1538)	61.6/60.9 (1565/1547)	61.6/60.9 (1565/1547)
Length	175.1 (4448)	175.1 (4448)	175.6 (4459)	175.6 (4459)
Width	75.7 (1924)**	75.7 (1924)**	75.2 (1911)**	75.2 (1911)**
Reported weight	3476lb (1577kg)	3319lb (1505kg)	3410 (1546kg)****	3441 (1561kg)
Ground clearance*	5.0 (127)	5.0 (127)	5.125 (130)	5.125 (130)
Legroom	42.6 (1082)	42.6 (1082)	42.4 (1077)	42.4 (1077)
Shoulder room	53.8 (1366)	53.8 (1366)	54.1 (1375)	54.1 (1375)
Trunk size	11.8cf (334L)	6.8cf (193L)***	8.4cf (238L)	n/a
Fuel	22gal (83L)	19gal (72L)	18.5gal (70L)	16gal (61L)
Oil	9qt (8.5L)	8qt (7.6L)	10.5qt (9.9L)	11qt (10.4L)
Coolant	19qt (18L)	12.8qt (11.9L)	12.8qt (11.9L)	16qt (15L)

* At design load
** At the window frame, 1993-2002; at the door sills, 2003-06
*** The 1996 RT/10 cargo space was listed at 3.6cf (102L) which was likely an error.
**** A 2006 Dodge brochure listed the Viper SRT10 as weighing 3436lb.

COUPE SPECIFICATIONS

	1996	**2006**	**2009**	**2015**
Wheelbase	96.2 (2444)	98.8 (2510)	98.8 (2510)	98.8 (2510)
Track w(F/R)	59.6/60.6 (1514/1538)	61.6/60.9 (1565/1547)	61.6/60.9 (1565/1547)	62.9/61.0 (1598/1550)
Length	175.1 (4448)	175.6 (4459)	175.6 (4459)	175.7 (4463)
Width	75.7 (1924)	75.2 (1911)	75.2 (1911)	76.4 (1941)
Curb weight	3383lb (1535kg)	3453 (1565)	3454 (1567)*	3390 (1537)**
Ground clearance	5.0 (127)	5.125 (130)	5.125 (130)	5.0 (127)
Legroom	42.6 (1082)	42.4 (1077)	42.4 (1077)	42.7 (1085)
Shoulder room	53.8 (1366)	54.1 (1375)	54.1 (1375)	53.1 (1348)
Trunk size	9.2cf (260L)	6.25cf (179L)	n/a	14.65cf (415L)
Fuel tank	19gal (72L)	18.5gal (70L)	16gal (61L)	16gal (61L)
Oil	8qt (7.6L)	10.5qt (9.9L)	11qt (10.4L)	11qt (10.4L)
Coolant	12.8qt (11.9L)	12.8qt (11.9L)	16qt (15L)	16qt (15L)

3408lb (1552kg) ACR, 3366lb (1533) ACR Hard Core

** 3390 (1537) base, 3366 (1526) with Sidewinder II wheels, 3390 (1537) Viper TA, 3415 (1549) GTS, 3399 (1541) GTS with Sidewinder II wheels*

TRANSMISSION GEARING

	1st	**2nd**	**3rd**	**4th**	**5th**	**6th**	**Axle**
1992-2006	2.66	1.78	1.30	1.00	0.74	0.50	3.07
2007-09	2.66	1.82	1.30	1.00	0.74	0.50	3.07
2010	2.66	1.82	1.30	1.00	0.80*	0.50	3.07
2013-16	2.26	1.58	1.19	1.00	0.77	0.50/0.63**	3.55

* Specifically, 0.796:1; this change was based on track experience, but cut 0-200mph (322km/h) acceleration time by 14 seconds, according to the press release.

** 0.50 in GT and GTS, 0.63 in Viper*

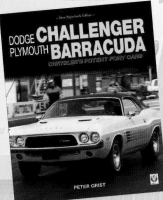

A living legend ...

... from the first, to the last.

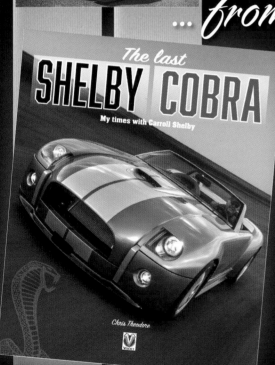

The last Shelby Cobra

My times with Carroll Shelby

Carroll Shelby, legendary driving ace, race team owner, and designer of Shelby Cobra, Daytona, and Mustang GT350 classics is revered by automotive enthusiasts, yet little has been written about the last quarter century of Carroll Shelby's life. During that time Chris Theodore, VP at Chrysler and Ford, developed a close personal friendship with Carroll.

The last Shelby Cobra chronicles the development of the many vehicles they worked on together (Viper, Ford GT, Shelby Cobra Concept, Shelby GR1, Shelby GT500 and others). It is an insider's story about how Shelby came back to the Ford family, and the intrigue behind the five-year journey to get a Shelby badge on a Ford Production Vehicle.

The author provides fresh insight and new stories of Shelby's larger-than-life personality, energy, interests and the many unpublished projects Carroll was involved with, up to his passing. Finally, the book describes their unfinished project, the Super Snake II Cobra, and the serendipitous circumstances that allowed to the author to acquire 'Daisy,' the last Shelby Cobra. To his many fans, Carroll Shelby was truly 'the most interesting man in the world.' ISBN: 9781787114500

INDEX